HOW TO BUY AND/OR SELL A SMALL BUSINESS FOR MAXIMUM PROFIT

A Step-by-Step Guide with Companion CD-ROM

By Rene' V. Richards

HOW TO BUY AND/OR SELL A SMALL BUSINESS FOR MAXIMUM PROFIT—A Step-by-Step Guide with Companion CD-ROM

ISBN-13: 978-0-910627-53-5   ISBN-10: 0-910627-53-3

Library of Congress Cataloging-in-Publication Data

Richards, Rene' V., 1965-
  How to buy and or sell a small business for maximum profit : a step-by-step guide / Rene' V. Richards.
      p. cm.
  Includes index.
  ISBN-13: 978-0-910627-53-5 (alk. paper)
  ISBN-10: 0-910627-53-3
  1. Sale of small businesses. 2. Business enterprises--Purchasing. 3. Small business. I. Title.

  HD62.7.R535 2006
  658.1'64--dc22
                          2006013810

ART DIRECTION, INTERIOR DESIGN & PRODUCTION: Lisa Peterson, Michael Meister • info@6sense.net
EDITOR: Jackie Ness • jackie_ness@charter.net; Wanda Morgan • wbmorgan@adelphia.net

Printed in the United States

CHAPTER 1: THE NOVICE ENTREPRENEUR: UNDERSTANDING YOURSELF

In order to succeed at any given business, you must first understand yourself in a business environment. What are your requirements as a buyer and/or seller? What situation fits your individual goals, objectives, and career assets? Are you flexible, adaptable, and an "outside the box" individual? Or are you happier with an environment that is structured and routine and offers very few surprises? A successful entrepreneur is an individual who is well-acquainted with his or her own individual strengths and weaknesses.

CHAPTER 2: THE BUSINESS

Once you're comfortable with your self-assessment and you know what you're looking for, where do you locate your potential business? Or if you're an already-established business person, how do you determine when your business might become profitable?

CHAPTER 3: THE STRATEGIES

Chapter 3 takes a look at the buying and selling strategies that are most successful and gives an overview of each situation.

From buying to marketing, there are proven methods that will work to make you profitable.

CHAPTER 4: THE EVALUATION

Whether you are buying or selling, you need to know the condition of the business you're examining. What are the economic circumstances surrounding the business? Market share, economic factors, growth opportunities, and the marketability of the business are crucial pieces of the buy/sell proposal. An in-depth understanding of all the circumstances is necessary if you are to achieve maximum profitability. The financial health of the business should be examined in conjunction with the economic health of the business. Asset value, income capitalization, cash flow, and retained earnings will give you a clearer picture of a few previous quarters of operation and the effect the management and surrounding economics has had on the business.

CHAPTER 5: THE VALUE OF A BUSINESS

This is the area where many potential buyers and sellers fail to spend enough time or do their homework. You must have extensive knowledge of the value of real estate prices in the surrounding area, new/used equipment pricing, the condition of the proposed business, and an estimated average of repair/reconditioning expense that is associated with a particular business during a buy or sell. If the business provides a service, how much of the potential value is leaving with the former owner? How much of the valuation is based on previous sales and potential sales? All of these factors must be considered when pricing a business, regardless of whether you are the buyer or the seller.

CHAPTER 6: THE PROFIT

If you're a buyer, the profit levels are as much of a concern for you as they are for the seller; any profit to be had will quite naturally increase the buying or selling price, depending upon your position. If you're the seller, this is money in your pocket; if you're the buyer, a greater investment will be required, usually equating to additional capital.

CHAPTER 7: THE CAPITAL AND FINANCING OPTIONS

The meat and potatoes of the deal: the capital required for the buy or sell. Capital can be obtained from several different sources; it is up to you, as the buyer, to seek out the available funding opportunities and then pursue your options. Quite often, there is the option of seller-financing; this will generally require an up-front equity investment on the part of the buyer, but it is sometimes the most feasible approach. Other options include venture capital, lending institutions, and/or SBA-approved funding.

CHAPTER 8: THE NEW BEGINNING: BUSINESS ORGANIZATION, LEGAL DOCUMENTS, AND TAX ISSUES

This chapter rolls all of the paper requirements into one chapter simply because these areas are so closely tied to each other, and they will normally need to be completed simultaneously. The one exception would be the letter of intent; all other legal, tax, and buy/sell documents are very interrelated and come one right after the other. Tax issues, capital gains, capital investments, retained earnings, profit and loss, legal business forms, and individual business tax and licensing issues are all covered in this chapter.

CHAPTER 9: THE DEAL

Negotiating the deal is one of the most important aspects of the buy/sell process. The art of negotiation and the skill needed to close with the best deal possible are valuable assets; and as a buyer/seller, if you don't possess them, look for a way to hire someone who does have them. This chapter covers all aspects of negotiation, structuring, non-compete clauses, letters of intent, and the closing process.

CHAPTER 10: THE TRANSITION

Once the deal is complete, what next? The period of transition and the required input from both the seller and buyer are often overlooked as part of the buy/sell agreement. However, a smooth transition period can greatly benefit each party, especially in the area of employee and existing-business retention.

CHAPTER 11: THE REALITY

In this final chapter, I'm going to tell you a few of the realities of business entrepreneurship that you don't learn in a book, the things that you're going to experience and live if you have the opportunity to sit in the driver's seat. The entrepreneurial position isn't for everyone; it takes a special someone to be an entrepreneur.

CONTENTS

PART II: The Journey

CHAPTER 4: THE EVALUATION   97

CHAPTER 5: THE VALUE OF A BUSINESS   133

CHAPTER 6: THE PROFIT   159

CHAPTER 7: THE CAPITAL AND FINANCING OPTIONS   171

PART III: The Realization

CHAPTER 8: THE NEW BEGINNING: BUSINESS ORGANIZATION, LEGAL DOCUMENTS, AND TAX ISSUES   195

CHAPTER 9: THE DEAL   207

CHAPTER 10: THE TRANSITION   233

CHAPTER 11: THE REALITY   243

CONCLUSION   253

APPENDIX A: GLOSSARY   255

APPENDIX B: CONFIDENTIALITY AGREEMENT   263

APPENDIX C: LETTER OF INTENT   265

APPENDIX D: PROPOSAL LETTER   269

APPENDIX E: SELLING MEMORANDUM   271

APPENDIX F: PURCHASE AND SELL AGREEMENT   275

APPENDIX G: REFERENCES   277

INDEX   279

AUTHOR BIOGRAPHY   284

P

Business owners will invariably tell you that owning your own business is one of the most challenging and rewarding positions you will ever hold. Would they do it again? Some would. Some would not.

As for me, I now delight in occupying the spectator's chair. Just as the athlete retires to the role of sports commentator and no longer actively participates in the sport, I have found an undeniable satisfaction in watching from the sidelines, evaluating, discussing, and analyzing. There is no greater joy for me than to observe a beginner in the game.

The zeal for success and the gleam of desire are always a part of a beginning player's attire.

I have participated in more business ventures than I care to recount; and at the end of the day, I was as much in love with the idea of the business as I had been at the beginning. I hope this book will serve as inspiration as well as guidance for the novice entrepreneur who is embarking on the journey of a lifetime.

F

One of the most challenging and rewarding steps
that an individual can take towards fulfilling the
dream of financial and creative freedom is to start,
buy, or operate their own business. The journey of a thousand
miles begins with the first step, but that first step can be an
overwhelming challenge without the knowledge you need to
complete the journey.

Business ownership is one of those tremendously rewarding,
yet often overwhelming journeys. Locating the information you
will need to make the journey a success is often quite difficult
and time consuming. This book provides the reader with the
information necessary to take an idea from conception to
completion in a successful and self-satisfying journey.

One of the most important steps an individual will take
begins with an "examination of self"; readers that utilize the
information in this publication will find that they have already
taken the first step to success and have the necessary tools at
their fingertips to successfully finish.

In my position as Vice President of Human Resources, I am in
contact with individuals of every description and within every
discipline which cause me to address the following issues most

frequently. How does the organization:

1. Implement and manage change,

2. Design the organization to be the most efficient,

3. Develop people in order to achieve business goals, and

4. Determine the metrics by which success should be measured.

These issues are essential to achieve sustained business growth and plan for future expansion. This publication provides one of the most effective methods for managing not only the business, but the resources necessary for success and evaluating the business for potential profitability.

Denise Starcher, MBA, SPHR, is currently the Vice President of Human Resources for a web services and consulting company headquartered in Atlanta, GA. She is an innovative HR professional with expertise in change management, organizational effectiveness, employee relations, compensation and benefits, and training and development. For the past 18 years, she has focused on enabling organizations to achieve sustained business growth while embracing change in the technology, hospitality, healthcare, and energy industries. She holds an MBA in General Management from Georgia State University, and a Bachelor of Science degree in Psychology from Centre College in Danville, Kentucky.

DEDICATION

D

THIS WORK COULD NOT HAVE BEEN COMPLETED WITHOUT THE INPUT AND HELP OF MANY INDIVIDUALS; HOWEVER, THERE ARE A FEW THAT MERIT A WORD OF PERSONAL THANKS...

TO MY FATHER, AN ENTREPRENEUR SINCE THE 3RD GRADE, AND THE ROOT OF MY BUSINESS INSPIRATION;

TO MY MOTHER, THE MOST CREATIVE AND INNOVATIVE PERSON I KNOW;

TO MY HUSBAND, FOR PROVIDING THE MOST ENCOURAGING AND LOVING SUPPORT I'VE EVER KNOWN;

TO DONNA, THE GREATEST BUSINESS PARTNER A GAL COULD EVER HAVE;

AND TO MY SON, WHO HAS GIVEN ME A REASON TO GET UP EACH DAY, FOR THE LAST 20 YEARS.

INTRODUCTION

I

- *Are you ready to embark on the journey of a lifetime?*
- *Do you have the stamina, drive, and desire to become a member of a rare breed?*
- *Statistically, you won't make it.*
- *Objectively, it will be the hardest thing you've ever done.*
- *Realistically, only a rare few are true business entrepreneurs.*
- *It's the American dream.*
- *So how badly do you want it?*

As you rise to the occasion and prepare to embark, you're going to need the necessary tools: information, observation, and orientation. The wonderful thing about these tools is that they're good for the entire journey. You'll use them throughout, and they work whether you're evaluating yourself, the business, or the competition.

This book starts at the beginning. There's no way to buy or sell a business until you know yourself as a businessperson. Once you have a clear picture of your strengths, weaknesses, likes, dislikes, personality style, management style, and tangible and intangible assets, you can begin to look at your business options. It does you no good to locate a business that you're not prepared to buy, sell, or operate.

Once you've successfully evaluated the "self" of this equation, you're ready to locate a business, examine buy-and-sell strategies, evaluate the health and finances of the business, and move toward the assessment of profit potential, investment of capital, and the actual realization of the dream of buying, owning, and/or selling a business.

Hopefully you will find direction, guidance, and some humor in these pages; and at the end, you will find yourself prepared to become one of a rare breed, a true business entrepreneur.

PART I

THE
DREAM

CHAPTER 1

THE NOVICE ENTREPRENEUR: UNDERSTANDING YOURSELF

The key issues addressed in Chapter 1 are the following:

- *Your Profile as a Buyer and/or Seller*
- *Personal Characteristics*
- *Individual Goals and Objectives*
- *Your Personal Resource*

In order to succeed at any given business, the first building block should be an understanding of yourself in a business environment. What are your requirements as a buyer and/or seller? What situation fits your individual goals, objectives, and career assets?

Are you flexible, adaptable, and an "outside the box" individual? Or are you happier with an environment that is structured and routine and offers very few surprises? A successful entrepreneur is an individual well-acquainted with his or her own individual strengths and weaknesses.

PERSONAL CHARACTERISTICS

Regardless whether you are a buyer or seller, there are certain characteristics that will help to make your journey a successful one. What are the characteristics most often associated with successful business owners? We list the most common here and offer a brief discussion of each in the following paragraphs.

1. Self-starter

2. Highly motivated

3. Multi-talented

4. Excellent leader

5. Flexible and adaptable

If you will take the time to perform the self-assessment, you may make some surprising discoveries, not the least of which might be your next entrepreneurial step. Whether you are a buyer, seller, or current owner, developing a greater understanding of you, your goals, and objectives as well as your strengths and weaknesses, only serves to make you a more knowledgeable individual.

Self-starters and highly motivated people have half the battle won when they start. The first few years of business ownership are grueling, hard, and often a test of will. The ability to show up every day for sixteen hours a day just because not showing up is not an option can test anyone's limits. It is during these days (when "the will to survive and thrive" is the only reason you can find to make it another day) that you must possess the motivation and desire to continue. I don't believe there's a successful first-generation business owner anywhere who is not in possession of this one characteristic; it will get you through the rough spots and help you to persevere in order to see the dream to culmination.

Multi-talented has everything to do with your position as an owner, leader, and manager. You will find at some point that you are everything to everyone. Hopefully, you won't have to fill all these shoes at once; but over the life of the business, you will wear many different hats and be many things to the employees, vendors, and customers with whom you do business. You will discover as you begin that you will need knowledge of every facet of the business you're in. The only way to gain that knowledge is to work with a particular department or area. You need to understand job requirements, information requirements, information output, and individual costs associated with individual areas; and you will need to perform an analysis of productivity and efficiency. Incidentally, you will need to do all of this while you fill the role of CEO, CIO, and owner. Your role as a leader will infiltrate and penetrate every level of the operation.

Leadership of the company and the employees will consume more of you and your abilities than we can possibly cover in this section. We touch on the subject of management again in Chapter 10, but it does not begin to discuss all the information you will need in order to be an effective leader and manager. I would recommend, however, that you check out some of the great books on management, management practices, and management theories available at any bookstore prior to finishing this book.

Flexibility and adaptability seem to work as a team, no matter where you find them. You will need to become an Olympic gymnast of sorts, bending, giving, twisting, changing, moving, and rearranging much of your life, your habits, your view of job requirements, and, last but not least, your personal life. The ability not only to change but to welcome change is as important as your possession of the ability to be a self-starter and to be motivated

We've discussed the characteristics of the more successful business owners, and while it is true that these are general characteristics, there are buyers and sellers that defy all normal benchmarks. The spirit of the individuals, their goals and objectives, and their resources also play a huge role in the successful business venture. As you evaluate yourself and review your business profile, you should remember that the modern-day entrepreneur is comparable to the Spanish explorers, Christopher Columbus, the religious immigrants, and the pioneers of early America.

A successful entrepreneur is an individual
well-acquainted with the assumption of risks,
the search for freedom, and the desire for independence.

INDIVIDUAL GOALS AND OBJECTIVES

You must have a clear understanding of your goals and business objectives at the outset. When you begin with a plan that adequately defines where you want to go and why, you are very likely to arrive at your destination with a great story to tell. You predetermine your fate if you have no clear objective, and you certainly aren't in a position to lead others. As a business owner, you are the captain of the ship; it will be your responsibility to guide and direct your employees.

If you will take a week and write down the following questions and answer them honestly, you will be in a position to set your goals and objectives from a realistic point of view, with the ability to realize and achieve. Many startup businesses simply lack the knowledge and experience that are needed to truly appreciate sales forecasts, pre-planned budgeting, and business plans. With this in mind, a clear understanding of your own goals and objectives will often mean the difference between success and failure.

There are many motivators for making the decision to buy or sell a business, and you need to fully understand yours. Freedom, independence, wealth, creativity, the chance to make a difference in your community, or the opportunity to work with cutting-edge technology are some of the most-often-cited reasons; however, the objective here is to determine *your* reason. If you're currently in business, why do you want to sell? Have you given any thought to what your direction will be after the sale?

If freedom and independence are your reasons for business ownership, what will it take for you to feel that you've accomplished that objective? If retirement is the objective, what is it that you hope to achieve as a retired individual? Do you feel comfortable with a highly structured environment, or are you seeking freedom and independence through an environment that offers lots of flexibility and adaptability? If wealth is your objective, what level of wealth will signal success? Do you need several million, or maybe only one or two? If creativity is your objective, how do you intend to incorporate the creative freedom you desire into your proposed buy or sale? The answers here aren't meant to be lengthy essays; simple, concise, and direct answers that establish your objectives are all that you need.

At what level are you comfortable in joining the business community? It's comparable to a swimmer. If you're a novice swimmer, start at the shallow end. If you're an expert swimmer, jump into the deep end. Understanding your limitations, your strengths, and your weaknesses will help you in determining where you stand in the business arena. This is a crucial step in your self-evaluation. Take enough time to accurately and objectively assess your comfort zone. Let me also say here that a true businessperson is never 100 percent comfortable with all the aspects of a business; a little discomfort will keep you alert! Stepping into business ownership is quite a leap within itself; you don't want to bite off more than you can comfortably chew. If you're at the point of leaving the business community as a seller, where do you begin in preparing yourself and at what level will you leave? Do you want to exit as an owner or stay on as a business consultant?

How to get there will come in the form of a business plan if you're buying (or a selling memorandum if you're selling), but for now, put together a brief timeline that clearly states your starting point, your business goals, your personal goals in relation to the business goals, and a brief review of how you intend to accomplish those goals. When you take the time to do a step-by-step guide of your intentions—your goals and objectives—you will sometimes discover that you are not as clear as you thought yourself to be and that your resources and experience may not be all you need to get you where you want to go.

Make a list in the very beginning of people you can call on, persons who are trusted mentors, advisors, and experts in some area of business. You will need trusted associates, a strong marriage (if you're married), and understanding friends. No entrepreneurial effort has ever achieved its greatest potential on one man's (or woman's) efforts alone. You cannot be an expert in all the areas where you will need a working knowledge in order to succeed. Establishing an active network of business associates, family members, and peers will only enhance your level of success.

YOUR PERSONAL RESOURCES

I saved this topic as the final area of review in your assessment of your personal business profile for a reason. Available resources are truly a necessity, but without an adequate understanding of yourself, your resources, both the tangible ones and the intangible ones, will not help you determine your path. Now that you have established your motives, goals, and objectives and have taken an accurate assessment of your business characteristics, you can successfully evaluate your arsenal of resources as they relate to your business profile.

You've now taken a look at your individual goals and objectives; there is, however, one more area that will greatly influence the goals and objectives you establish and will play a major role in your ability to succeed: your family. What role does your family play in your personal life? To what extent do your family and personal life influence your business life? You will need answers to these questions. Sit down with your family and discuss the possibility of buying a business and the effect it might have on your personal life. Your role as a father, mother, or spouse will most surely be affected, and you (as well as your family) need to be prepared for these changes. You can rest assured that the purchase and operation of a business will be a test of your relationship with your family and a testament to your strength and devotion if you survive with your family intact.

A resource can be defined as a limited supply of an asset with economic value. You have two sets: intangible and tangible. Intangible assets can't really be seen, moved, sold, or even adequately assessed with a value. But they are valuable nonetheless and therefore just as important as a resource. Your skills and business experience are your intangible assets. The tangible resources are, of course, resources you can physically see, move, touch, and assess with a value. Your tangible resources include your investment capital, cash flow, and professional advisors for different areas of the business process.

What about your skills? What do you bring to the table in a skills assessment? Your skills are basically a statement of your capabilities. What can you do as a business owner that would contribute to the success of the business? Managerial knowledge and skills, situational analysis, and business knowledge are the most desirable skills you could possess; they're not, however, the only skills you might possess. The ability to manage people, quickly assess a situation or analyze a process, and a varied array of business knowledge will see you through the majority of everyday business situations. The skills you possess are as important as the characteristics you need. Take a moment to do a skills and work experience inventory. Start with a clean sheet of paper. Make a list of your skills and experience; if you've worked as a business professional, you will more than likely have a résumé. Review the information on your résumé; it is an effective statement of your work- and business-related skills as well as your work experience. Now build on that information. You might be surprised at the results.

What about your experience? Where have you spent most of your adult working life? Over the course of your life, you learn from your mistakes, you learn from those around you, and you learn from business situations and exposure. Many of the managerial courses that are taught rely on day-to-day situations in the workplace to effectively communicate certain techniques. You accumulate experience as you accumulate age and live your life. Many times, this can prove to be a most valuable asset, especially when running a business; juggling different personalities, stressful environments, and customer deadlines can prove overwhelming without some prior experience.

Your tangible resources would be assets necessary for the actual financing of the business. What, specifically, are those assets? A general definition of those resources would be investment capital or owner equity, adequate cash flow for operations, trusted professional advisors, and the time necessary to bring the dream to realization. We're going to take a brief look at each of these resources as they will be covered in more detail during later chapters.

Investment capital or owner equity is the investment you have available to put into the business you're looking to buy. Generally, investment capital is cash or stock. However, this is not necessarily the case; your investment may be in the form of equipment, machinery, land, or buildings. The investment capital should be an item or items that would be needed by the business and add value to the business. Generally, lending institutions, venture capitalists, and any other institution in the business of providing financing for business purchases will require that you, as the buyer, make an investment in the business also. The general rule of thumb will be a required buyer investment of around 10 to 20 percent of the assessed value of the business.

Adequate cash flow for the business is an often overlooked but crucial part of business operations. It is often overlooked because this resource is not cash you're going to necessarily have to put into the business but is more of an emergency buffer. If, for instance, the business you purchase does not initially produce enough to maintain an adequate cash flow, then the needed shortfall must come from you, the buyer. Many businesses fail because of a lack of adequate cash flow for the first few months. I have heard numerous associates lament, "If only there had been enough cash to get the business through the three months of declining sales, we would have made it." It can be a make-or-break issue.

There cannot be enough emphasis placed on professional advisors who can provide trusted, unbiased, objective advice. There are so many different pieces of the puzzle when you set out to buy a business: accounting, legal, tax, business organization, management, and employee issues, just to name the most common. You are a business owner; you're not an accountant, a lawyer, or a human resources manager. Yet you're going to need advice and input in all of these areas. Three of the greatest concerns are accounting, tax, and legal issues. Making the right choices from the very beginning based on accurate and reliable information will chart your course for the first five years of your business operations. Your greatest responsibility at this point is to find the right people to provide the right advice and information.

CASE STUDY

CBC Bookkeeping and Tax Service is an accounting and bookkeeping service that provides local customers with professional tax services as well as an on-call personal advisor.

Contact Information: Rene' V. Richards
1096 Mt. Pleasant Ch. Rd
Millport, AL 35576

I became a small business owner to provide my family's businesses with their needed bookkeeping services. Furthermore, I truly enjoy bookkeeping and accounting, so starting a bookkeeping and tax service was a natural choice. It's also given me the opportunity to play an important role in the operation of our family's businesses and to grow my own business. My prior experience in the restaurant/store business, my accounting background, and my marketing skills all contributed to my success. My partner also was very dedicated and had an excellent work ethic.

Business-wise, operating an accounting and tax service has been an excellent extra income business, and it has now grown into a full-time business.

Of course, it takes long hours and hard work to build a successful business. Additionally, the building of a loyal customer base in this line of work is a long and difficult process. However, I believe I've been able to provide a needed service to several business customers that has helped them to achieve success.

For some business owners, there comes a time when it's just time to move on. When I sold a business, I used a combination of two methods (EBIT and an asset-based valuation) to value the business. I've actually financed the sale of a business with a seller-financed mortgage. One of the key components of a successful sale is you have to trust the individual you're selling the business to, and you have to believe they will succeed. When I sold my business, I was actually approached from someone interested in purchasing it.

When I purchased my business, I used seller financing options, sought out other forms of financing, and performed due diligence prior to my purchase. I had no reservations about the purchase. We first leased the business to determine the validity of the sales volume; negotiated a buy price with the seller; and asked for a certain percentage of seller financing.

CLASSIFIED CASE STUDIES™
directly from the experts

I used a local banker to handle the legal details while I took care of all of the tax issues.

I would absolutely recommend starting a business. It's the best wealth-building option, other than investing, available to individuals today.

THE BUSINESS

Key issues covered in Chapter 2 will be:

- *Motives, Expectations, and Risk*
- *Personal Preparation*
- *Establishing Purchasing/Selling Criteria*
- *Locating a Potential Business*
- *Putting Together a Search Plan*
- *Hiring an Intermediary*
- *Knowing When to Buy or Sell*

MOTIVES, EXPECTATIONS, AND RISKS

Once you're comfortable with your self-assessment, you can establish your search criteria. The most successful method for locating a potential business, whether for sale or purchase, is to first establish definitive search criteria and then to establish your relationship with a person known as an intermediary. You will benefit tremendously when you hire a company or individual that locates and evaluates businesses as a profession. Even if you have already identified a possible business for purchase, it is in your best interest to retain a professional. You will need someone whose job it is to watch the market;

evaluate businesses; provide reliable, sound second opinions; and act as your guide through the buying or selling process. Locating a business to purchase or preparing a business for sale is sometimes a lengthy process, and there are several different phases that you will complete before arriving at your final destination.

There are traditionally three different types of businesses to buy: cash cows, growth companies, or turnaround companies. Cash cows are businesses that have a steady cash flow and are well-established and competitive in a strong market. Growth companies have begun to see or are expected to begin to see increasing revenues and profits. If you're interested in purchasing a growth company, you will more than likely pay a premium price. The last alternative is a turnaround company. These are companies that have experienced some sort of difficult times, usually financial. Turnaround companies can often be bought at a great price, but they're not going to be easy to turn around. It will take extraordinary leadership.

What do you expect from your business in relation to the effort you will invest? In other words, you only get out of something what you put into it. If you're looking for a business that will require very little active effort from you, then you need to make that a part of your search criteria. The same concept may also apply to your search efforts. If time constraints are a concern, then you must be prepared to take a more active role in the search for the right business or buyer.

Deciding how much risk you can comfortably live with is where you must be brutally honest with yourself and your guidelines in developing your search plan. Some businesses may offer an opportunity for tremendous returns, but they may be in a very risky, unstable market segment. Can you accept those conditions? If so, you're ready to move; if not, then you might want to decline this opportunity and wait until it's safe and sure. This assessment of your motives, expectations, and risks will place you, generally, in one of three categories: serious and realistic, casual and realistic, or unrealistic.

- **Serious and realistic.** This category, whether you're a buyer or seller, fits the truly dedicated and sincere individual — someone willing to dedicate the necessary time, resources, and patience to fulfill the search.

- **Casual and realistic.** Individuals in this category are involved only if the process is fairly simple and straightforward. They won't walk away from a great deal, but they're not going to spend a great amount of time to locate one, either.

- **Unrealistic.** These individuals are simply waiting for the "deal of a lifetime" to drop from the sky. A word of realism: they will still be waiting when the sky drops.

In-depth understanding of your profile as a buyer or seller and as a searcher has prepared you for the next step, developing your individual purchasing or selling criteria. This leads to the development of the complete search plan.

PERSONAL PREPARATION

Regardless whether you are a buyer or a seller, there must be some degree of personal preparation for a journey so monumental. There are decisions to be made, both on a personal and family level, that require serious thought and reflection, input from other members of your family, and an evaluation of your personal life. As with your discovery of your buy/sell profile, you need to establish your buy/sell criteria. What boundaries can you live with? What boundaries and limits can your family live with? Before you can effectively proceed, you must establish purchasing and selling criteria.

ESTABLISHING PURCHASING/SELLING CRITERIA

Individual Purchase Criteria

In Chapter 1, you established your profile as a buyer or seller and determined your strengths and weaknesses, goals and objectives, and available resources; now, armed with that information, you need to identify your individual buying or selling criteria. Take a look around. What do you want in a business? What are you looking for? The answers to some general questions will aid you in determining the direction for the remainder of the search process as well as for the persons aiding you in that search.

1. What type of business am I interested in buying?

2. What type of business am I most suited to operate?

3. What kind of individual should I look for to help me?

4. What type of advice will I need in order to develop a buying situation?

5. Which type of strategy will I use in buying a business?

6. What level of investment can I afford?

7. Can I secure financing for a business purchase?

Individual Selling Criteria

Establishing your individual selling criteria will follow much the same questioning as the purchasing criteria.

1. What type of business am I selling?

2. Where will I find purchasing candidates?

3. What kind of individual should I look for to help me?

4. What type of advice will I need in order to develop a selling situation?

5. Which type of strategy will I use in selling a business?

6. Am I willing to finance any part of the sell?

7. Am I willing to remain with the new owners for a certain length of time?

These questions are individually addressed throughout the rest of Chapters 2, 3, 4, and 5.

Try to remember as you answer these questions that buying or selling a business is a work in progress. It will usually take six months to two years to move through the entire process. There may be times when you need to reassess your criteria. Some piece or part of the objective may change; if so, you'll need to reevaluate your position. Don't be hesitant to do just that. A note of extreme importance: You must live with the end result; make sure it's a result you want to live with.

One other important point to make at this juncture: It matters not whether you are a buyer or a seller, you are the captain of this journey; maintain your focus throughout the entire process, exercise patience, and define the necessary course of action.

LOCATING A POTENTIAL BUSINESS

Today's business market is comprised of four different types of businesses: manufacturing, distribution, retail, and service. If you've accurately answered your self-analysis questions and the purchasing/selling criteria in the previous section, you probably already know which of these industries interests you and why. But for the sake of discussion, let's take a brief look at each one simply to confirm what you probably already know.

Manufacturing

A manufacturing business is simply that: it makes or manufactures a product. There are so many pieces to the manufacturing puzzle that unless you already have a background in it, I certainly would not recommend purchasing a manufacturing facility. This one is more than likely a buy only if you're absolutely certain you can wear the many hats you will need for day-to-day operations. If your intent is to run it in a hands-on manner, you need to take the business apart, area by area, and ascertain your level of knowledge and skill in each area. Purchasing, inventory, engineering, production, quality, shipping, accounting, and sales are the primary areas of concern, ones that will require some knowledge on your end. There are some other concerns that will be addressed later in Chapter 4 concerning the overall health of a business; the industry and the decision to purchase this type of industry will rely heavily on the information revealed as you complete the evaluation of the business.

Now, on a more optimistic note, there are some really good reasons to consider a manufacturing business. You are making something of your own: a product that can be uniquely yours. You have the opportunity to make your mark, to separate yourself from the competition and become an industry leader. You're also more the master of your destiny. You make the decisions and call the shots; if you're right about your sales and marketing campaigns, you can be extremely successful. And, with careful monitoring of your process, the profit margins are generally quite considerable in the field of manufacturing.

Distribution

Now here's a business that you can really sink your teeth into. Success in a distribution business depends heavily on the abilities of the owner. There's also the possibility that your predecessor's or successor's abilities and yours are vastly different. This can work for you or against you. At any rate, the distribution industry gives the person running the business a real opportunity to succeed without the overhead that a manufacturing business requires. You're also given a greater amount of customer interaction. If you enjoy people and like an ever-changing business environment, distribution would be worthy of your consideration. The drawback to distribution: your profits are small, and you are heavily dependent on the ability of your customers to stay current with their payments as well as their purchases. This is a riskier game than manufacturing, but the opportunity for growth and success are more a result of owner effort.

Retail

The retail industry is different. Retail sales is a labor-intensive, high-turnover, mixed-profit-margin, customer-reliant, fast-paced business. If you're up for a challenge and don't mind taking risks, this would be the business you need. This is also another one, like manufacturing, where if you don't have some sort of background and previous experience, I wouldn't recommend that you get into it. The learning curve when acquiring a retail business is short, in part because you don't have any security in your employee knowledge base nor any retention or loyalty; for the remaining part, you must be able to read your customers extremely well. Having what the customers want when they want it is the only way to succeed in retail sales. Sometimes this means you must be very perceptive and operate on intuition alone. Purchasing a retail business will also require large amounts of capital, especially if your purchase includes real estate, inventory, and customer accounts. But for the potential business owner who truly enjoys interaction with customers and a constantly changing environment, retail is the place to be. A word of caution when you consider the retail sales business: This industry is greatly affected by inflation, recession, and consumer opinion.

Service

Of all the industries, this one is probably the most often tried and the most often to fail. It generally is not because of a lack of knowledge on the part of the owner; it normally is a result of poor management and people skills. If you're anticipating purchasing this type of business, make sure that you either have extensive business knowledge or that you hire an excellent business manager. As a general rule, service providers are experts in the service they provide but not in the particular area of business, unless, of course, you're offering business services. Since you offer a service and not a product, you should make every effort to hire employees who will not steal customers and require that they sign non-compete agreements. The service industry has excellent profit margins and low overhead as long as you can keep your customers. It can be a very fickle market, heavily reliant on customer opinion.

Although family businesses cut across all the different categories listed above, they do merit some discussion during our examination of the four different types of business for one simple reason: They are in a class by themselves in that if you're considering the purchase or sale of a family business, there will be some special considerations for obtaining financial information and examining that information; and the valuation technique may be somewhat specialized since many family-owned small businesses do not typically allow cash to accrue in the business. There will typically be less management in place and a narrower customer base. At times, estate tax sales will offer excellent buyout opportunities. When the founder dies, small family-operated businesses are often not prepared for the onslaught of financial responsibilities, and cash flow often becomes a problem. Be wary of a family business where several family members are in a position to stop or temporarily suspend the sale of the business; this dissension could quickly ruin an excellent opportunity and put you months behind in your buying process.

Obtaining capital for an industry that you know well and already have an established successful reputation in will be much easier because you will probably already have an established relationship with potential customers and vendors and you already understand your market.

Although it will be discussed at greater length in the following section, the importance of industry knowledge, your background, and work experience should play a big role in your decision; this cannot be stressed enough.

Stay in the Industry That Matches Your Background

This is one of the most important points. Whether you are buying or selling, you should understand that if you cross into uncharted territory, take the necessary precautions and hire expert advice. The money you could potentially save might just mean the difference in failure or success. Why is this factor so important for success? Well, if you really stop to consider the ramifications of your choices, you won't need a scientist to tell you the "why" in this situation. If you intend to personally manage your business, you need to know as much as possible about the industry, the business you are buying, the economics of the area, and the management style most effective in this particular business. How do you absorb that much information that quickly? You don't. Therefore, if you don't have some prior knowledge or experience in the business you've just purchased, you cannot expect to be profitable for quite some time.

Now, if you purchase a business with the intention of hiring an onsite manager, you won't need as much hands-on experience. After all, you're hiring that; what you will need is to obtain as much information regarding the day-to-day operations as is available so you will be prepared to interact with the manager you've hired in making the right and most profitable business decisions.

Acquisition/Selling Criteria

Arming yourself with information, self-analysis, industry and trade publications, and a strong team of personal advisors will aid you during the creation of your detailed acquisition or selling criteria. Never miss the opportunity to gain information about a potential buy or sell situation; it might just fit your requirements down to the last letter. You won't be able to determine that fact, however, without first understanding those requirements.

Define the Acquisition Parameters

As you prepare yourself to begin a search and you are determining those parameters, remember that in any successful endeavor there is a well-put-together plan. Your search is no different. You need an organized plan to give you focus and to provide you, the entrepreneur, with direction during the process. An additional point of interest if you decide to work with an intermediary: He or she will expect you to provide this information, sometimes even prior to accepting your proposal. Almost everyone who you encounter during the different phases of a purchase will be more responsive and cooperative if you have established search parameters. Although the questions asked below are quite pointed, please try to keep your line of questioning as pertinent to your situation as possible. Having performed your self-evaluation, you may already have definitive answers to some of the following questions; however, in determining your acquisition parameters, you may need to exercise some flexibility and adaptability in order to achieve the ultimate goal.

How Much Time Are You Willing to Devote to Locating a Business?

As with any major decision or important milestone in a person's life, the decision to buy or sell a business can't be made overnight, and the entire process won't happen in a couple of weeks. You need to examine your life and determine the amount of time you can devote to your effort and whether or not your personal life will support such an endeavor. As an entrepreneur, you cannot split yourself between personal conflict and the pursuit of a dream. Success in the business world has often been dependent upon the attention, drive, and motivation of the business owner. You should expect your search to last from a very optimistic six months to a more realistic two years. If you can't financially afford this type of commitment or if you're not personally ready, I would suggest that you wait. It is much better to delay rather than to set yourself up for an immediate failure.

What Funds Are Available?

In addressing this question, you're not looking at borrowed funds; you need to ascertain what funds you currently have available to invest in a business purchase. No matter what endeavor you undertake, almost all potential lenders or investors want to know that you are a worthy risk. One of the best ways to establish your dedication and commitment and to obtain further funding is to invest your personal assets. The investment doesn't necessarily have to be cash; it can be any asset that will be needed by the proposed business. Customarily, however, an individual doesn't have equipment and machinery just sitting around in a warehouse.

How Much Do You Want to Spend?

This is a tremendously important question and one that will in large part determine what you buy. If you're only willing to spend a couple of hundred thousand, you don't need to worry about a manufacturing business. Not even failed companies can be purchased that cheaply. As you establish criteria, place emphasis on limits that are realistic yet affordable. You must understand that there are other considerations such as operating cash. Examine your personal financial information. Make sure that you have adequately assessed your available assets and investment levels and that you can comfortably afford the level you've set.

What Is the Desired Business?

After reading the information in the first few paragraphs of Chapter 2 and performing your personal assessment, you should have a fairly well-developed idea about the kind of business you are suited to purchase. You should be ready to decide whether you're going to be a hands-on manager and which business you're actually suited to run. Let me remind you again in case you need to hear this once more: You benefit by staying within an industry that you have knowledge in, work experience to draw from, or established contacts. This will make your efforts to purchase and your ability to value the business much easier.

How Much Risk Are You Willing to Assume?

That is a very difficult question to answer because it's very hard to determine the risk factors involved when purchasing a business. There are the evident risks of acquisition of capital, injury liabilities, and failed marketing campaigns. But what about the not-so-obvious risks like the economy? Are you willing to risk your business reputation or your personal wealth? Are your personal responsibilities too great at the moment to support a risky business purchase? Careful consideration and thought must be given to the level of risk you and your family can assume. And as in most situations, you must assume that something will go wrong at some point. Very few businesses operate under perfect circumstances over the entire life of the business.

Define the Selling Parameters

As you prepare yourself and your business to be sold, you will need to determine your selling requirements just as the buyer establishes acquisition requirements. You, too, will need an organized plan that will provide you with focus and direction. You, as a seller, will also be asked to answer many of the same questions that buyers are required to answer when approaching intermediaries and team advisors. If you want to obtain the most value possible from your sell, you must treat the sell as you would any other business decision: plan carefully, assess, and review.

Why Do You Want to Sell?

Why do you want to sell your business? That is going to be one of the first questions you will be asked by potential buyers, intermediaries, and anyone from whom you seek business advice. Be prepared to answer this question honestly after you have taken the time to determine the real answers. Sometimes business owners will answer that it is because of the money; but rarely is that the real, driving reason behind a business sale.

Are You Willing to Devote the Time Needed for the Sale?

As with any major decision or important milestone in a person's life, the decision to buy or sell a business can't be made overnight, and the entire process won't happen in a couple of weeks. You need to examine your life and determine the amount of time you can devote to your effort and if your personal life will support such an endeavor. As an entrepreneur, you cannot split yourself between personal conflict and the pursuit of a dream. The time commitment, regardless of your position as a buyer or seller, is an issue; it is an issue you must examine, and you must decide whether you can commit to it. Try to remember that you're talking about selling a business that will, in all probability, net you a six-figure profit. These transactions do not happen within a few days or even a few months. It will take you at least a year to ready your business for sale and then an additional year to locate a serious buyer.

Are You Looking for a Specific Type of Buyer?

Speaking of buyers, are you placing restrictions on the type of buyer you will sell to? Are you looking for a buyer who will readily replace yourself or one that will take the business in a completely different direction? When you sell a business, especially one you built from the beginning, you are protective of that business. Many owners won't sell unless they're confident the proposed buyer will take care of existing employees and exhibit a deep commitment to the success of the business.

Are You Willing to Finance?

This is a question that will often determine how quickly you find a buyer, and the type of buyer you find. Seller-financed mortgages are not that uncommon; and depending upon the buyer that you find, you may or may not offer this as an option. Quite often, if a business is sold to associates or family members, the seller will offer this type of financing. It does have its risks, however. There is the possibility that the new owner will ruin the business; and if so, you run the possibility of never receiving your money. The flip side to this type of financing: Sellers who offer financing find it harder to let go of a business, and new owners may find themselves struggling to run a business and also please an overbearing lender.

Are You Willing to Stay On?

In answering this question, you need to have an excellent understanding of yourself and your ability to turn over the control of your business to a new owner. If you're the kind of person who has difficulty letting someone else take the reins, you might want to omit this offer from your selling parameters. Although it can be an inducement in many instances for the buyer, it can also turn into a very difficult and strained work environment. Your experience and expertise can be a tremendous asset to a small business provided you and the new owner possess the ability to work cooperatively and recognize boundaries.

What Do You Expect from the Sale?

Have a clear picture of your expectations that includes profit, payout methods, and your final negotiation limitations. The more prepared you are for the terms of the sale, the easier it will be to locate a buyer and then conduct the negotiations. You're also better able to utilize a professional team of advisors if they, too, are aware of your expectations.

Once you've completed the specifics for your acquisition or selling criteria, you're ready to put together a structured search plan. The right plan, whether you're buying or selling, will prove a tremendous asset once you're engaged in the search itself. If you've taken the advice given here, you will seek out an intermediary as well as a team of professional advisors; if this is the case, they will not only want but need a written, structured search plan.

PUTTING TOGETHER A SEARCH PLAN

Your search plan doesn't have to be an elaborate, 100-page document; it simply needs to list, in some detail, your established search criteria from the previous chapter and the areas we've discussed up to this point in Chapter 2. I've provided a sample search plan below. I would encourage you to take a moment to review it, and when the time arrives that you're ready to put together your own plan, return once again to this sample. As you put together your own structured search plan, you may find it necessary to add or subtract certain categories, depending upon your situation. This is the purpose of the individualized plan. It must fit your particular search needs. It is not necessary to maintain a specific order; however, the order used below is reflective of the manner in which you may be asked this information when using intermediaries and other professional advisors.

SEARCH PLAN for _____

1. Type of Industry

    a._____

    b._____

2. Type of Business

    a._____

    b._____

3. Size of Business (in relation to investment capability)

4. Are you willing to relocate if necessary?

5. What are your geographical preferences?

    a._____

    b._____

    c._____

6. What is your risk level?

7. Do you want to actively manage, or will you be an absentee owner?

8. What are the time constraints for purchase completion?

Once you've put together your search plan, you might want to take a few moments to construct a table that lists possible contacts, possible businesses that fit your search criteria, tools that you could utilize during your search such as letters of introduction, and follow-up letters and phone calls. Developing an established formula for conducting your search will help to make the development of possible buyers become a methodical habit for you. Following an established method of contact, introduction, and follow-up will ensure that you are not guilty of letting opportunity slip through your fingers!

To follow is a sample table for listing the information referenced above. There are sample templates available in the appendices that can be used as letters of introduction, follow-up correspondence, and for telephone conversation notation. There is also a standard form for establishing procedures to apply to each possible candidate as you move through the process of locating a potential business.

Contact/ Networking	Phone Number/ Address	Date of Contact and Follow-Up

The use of timelines, charts, and tables doesn't end with the search-plan criteria. Once you have a search plan and are ready to actually begin your search, you may find that creating a PERT (Program Evaluation Review Technique) chart or timeline of events will also aid you in your search efforts. It can be a tremendous benefit if you are attempting to coordinate various individuals' responsibilities and deadlines for completion dates. These charts can be used in conjunction with the templates you use for each business or simply as an overall guide for project completion. Your best approach is simply to prepare a template that can be used in various areas and revised when necessary.

Week	Task	Est. Time to Complete	Notes	To Do	WIP*	C
1	Develop Criteria	5 Days			X	
	Prepare Search Plan	3 Days		X		
	Contact Advisors	5 Days		X		

* WIP=Work in Process

If all of this seems like a lot of paperwork that so far has not produced a live buyer, consider this: A structured search that utilizes the lists and tables described above will produce results in half the time of an unstructured random search. So take heart and invest the amount of time necessary to assess, evaluate, organize, and plan. This disciplined approach will benefit you now and in the future as a business owner, buyer, or seller. No matter what your approach, the use of the techniques given here will prove to be a tremendous benefit.

Your next step in putting together your plan should be to hire an intermediary. Think of the intermediary as equal to a general contractor hired to build a home. The general contractor oversees the entire building process, often contacting individual contractors when necessary and assuring the homeowner that building and zoning requirements are complied with and that the work is moving along according to the homeowner's specifications. This is exactly what an intermediary does in the business arena. Many times an individual will attempt to be business owner and general contractor at the same time. This never works as expected. Your safest and most profitable approach is to hire an intermediary.

HIRING AN INTERMEDIARY

Since the use of an intermediary is a generic need regardless of whether you are buying or selling, let's take a look at the role of the intermediary, the evaluation criteria, and your gut feeling when hiring an intermediary. Intermediaries may be referred to by several different titles; sometimes they're known as finders, brokers, or the term we're going to use—intermediary. After all, an intermediary is a person who intercedes on someone else's behalf, and that is exactly what you're hiring.

For evaluation and hiring purposes, let's take a more detailed look at the exact responsibilities an intermediary should shoulder and then determine how best to evaluate your specific needs. As you search for an intermediary, you may choose to take a more active role and designate some areas of responsibility as a joint effort between yourself and the intermediary. That's perfectly acceptable; the more active you are in your endeavor, the greater the chance of success.

What responsibilities do you want the intermediary to assume? Let's take a look at the more common ones and discuss them in detail.

As a Seller

The selling memorandum is perhaps one of the most important services the intermediary will provide. It provides the opportunity for you to package your business for sale in the best light possible. The descriptions and information you provide in the selling memorandum are the first glimpse a potential buyer will have of your company. It should make the best impression possible and entice the buyer to investigate further. This document will be covered in more detail later in this chapter under "Knowing When to Sell," but it is an extremely important document; your intermediary should be able to provide previous samples of his or her work.

Although your intermediary must work with a professional business appraiser, to construct a value and price range portfolio, this instrument will be a guide that is worth its weight in gold. This forms the basis by which you will judge all offers — the "gold" standard, so to speak. An intermediary will prove invaluable when it comes to establishing this guide. An experienced intermediary can take the information you provide via your self-evaluation and assessments and the information provided from a professional business appraiser and produce a document that clearly defines what you want, need, and will accept.

Locating and screening buyers is the point where the intermediary actually begins to resemble an "intermediate" person. At this juncture, the intermediary is armed with a selling memorandum that favorably describes your company and a value and price range portfolio that financially and monetarily describes it. With these in hand, it's time to go to work. Locating and screening potential buyers can be a long and difficult process. The more time an intermediary has to devote to your project, the better your chances for locating buyers faster.

Once your intermediary has the necessary information and has put together a sale package and forwarded it to potential serious buyers, it's now a game of wait and see. The intermediary will, of course, continue to work to find additional potential buyers, but neither buying nor selling a business is an overnight accomplishment. When the proposals to buy do begin to arrive, they should be screened and reviewed by the intermediary for validity. This saves you, the seller, precious time and will prove the best method for maintaining objectivity during the process. It is also crucial that the potential buyers be made aware of confidentiality issues and sign an agreement and that the information exchange be monitored. When an actual buyer is found, it is time to move to the next phase: negotiating and closing the deal.

It is absolutely crucial to be either an authority in negotiations or to use the services of someone who is an authority in negotiating and successfully closing the deal. This is the role your intermediary should play extremely well. Experience is often the best teacher, and so it is with negotiations. Successful negotiation is truly an art. From techniques used to time allotments, the true negotiator is the master. By controlling a seemingly uncontrollable process, the professional negotiator achieves victory. Your intermediary will be your staunchest ally during the negotiating and closing process; seek first the aid of professionals, and then allow them to do their jobs. The prepared intermediary is armed with the necessary information, a predetermined accept-or-reject price, and an estimated time frame for completing and closing the deal. The experienced and seasoned intermediary will portray an air of calmness and command no matter the surrounding environment or circumstances. By keeping a level head, staying mentally alert, and using the right negotiating techniques, the intermediary will be successful.

As a Buyer

Generally, when you hire professional intermediaries, they should be experienced in the types and availability of financing for business purchases. There are so many different ways to approach the financing of a business that often the intermediary is more familiar with the best options than either the buyer or the seller. Your intermediary should seek your best financing options: what will inevitably work in the buyer's favor at the least expense. Quite often, the financing plan for a buyout will entail more than just debt financing.

Experienced and seasoned professional intermediaries will not be in short supply of interested leads. More than likely, they are aware of a potential seller or a business that is already on the market that will fit your specified criteria. It is in this area that retaining the services of a professional intermediary can actually work to speed up the buying process and get the best deal for you as a buyer.

Suppose the criteria you have put together and given to your intermediary fits several companies already on the market. How do you put together a proposal that will intrigue the business owners? Your intermediary begins to really earn his or her retainer fee at this point. It is at this juncture that serious proposals and negotiations are about to begin; the intermediary with experience understands the importance of the relationship between the buyer and seller and the chemistry that must come together in order to close the deal. You and your intermediary must be very knowledgeable about the business in question, your acquisition proposal, and exactly where you can give and take.

It's very important that you take an active role in the due-diligence proceedings. I cannot stress this enough here; this is a part of the deal. When you enter into an agreement to purchase a business, you must be aware of the responsibilities and liabilities that you are acquiring. The performance of thorough due diligence will ensure that you aren't acquiring more liability than anticipated. There are three types of due diligence that should be performed, and they are discussed in detail in Chapters 4 and 5.

When it comes to negotiations and closing the deal, it is crucial that the intermediary be experienced. This is the role your intermediary should play extremely well, and experience is often the best teacher. From the techniques used to time allotments, the true negotiator is the master of the ring, and in so controlling a seemingly uncontrollable process achieves victory. Seek first the aid of a professional, and then allow him or her to do the job. The prepared intermediary is armed with the necessary information, a predetermined accept-or-reject price, and an estimated time frame for completing and closing the deal. As I also stated earlier, the experienced and seasoned intermediary will portray an air of calmness and command regardless of the surrounding environment or circumstances. Keeping a level head, staying mentally alert, and using the right negotiating techniques, the intermediary will be successful.

Evaluation Criteria for the Intermediary

There are some generic guides to use in determining the qualifications of the intermediary. However, the most qualified candidate is not always the right one. As you begin your search, take into consideration the following factors, but don't make your decision based on these factors alone. Meet with your candidate; determine if you have personalities that will allow you to work together well. Do your personalities and temperaments complement each other? This is just as important as the experience and knowledge the candidate possesses.

1. Check the most recent work experience.

2. Determine whether the intermediary possesses a personality that attracts people. Look for industry familiarity as well as relevant work experience.

3. Make certain the intermediary is focused and committed to your particular situation.

4. Ask questions that pertain to your industry as well as to the methods of valuation, negotiation, deal proposals, and business contacts.

5. If any of the information the intermediary provides seems unrealistic or incomplete, keep looking.

Sources for intermediaries include banks, merger-and-acquisition companies, real estate brokers, network contacts, and industry specialists. These individuals make their livings smoothing out the rough edges for buyers and sellers. If they are good at what they do, they will be worth more than you're going to pay them. If you do not choose wisely, however, your experience may be less than satisfying. Ultimately, it is up to you as the buyer or seller to make a wise choice and then live with that choice.

Once you've made your decision about your intermediary, if the situation warrants (in almost 100 percent of the cases I've seen, it does), you will need to work with your intermediary to put together an acquisition or advisory team. The people who serve as advisors in a buy/sell process are people who can actually make a viable and beneficial contribution to the process. In other words, you need people from whom you will receive a benefit—lawyers, tax attorneys, CPAs, business valuation experts, real estate appraisers, financiers, etc. These are individuals who serve as members of advisory teams, and if you choose wisely, their presence will benefit you greatly.

Advisory Team

The acquisition or advisory team will generally consist of lawyers, bankers, accountants, acquisitions consultants, and your intermediary. There are many reasons for actually hiring an acquisition or advisory team, but the greatest reason any individual should seek the help and advice of such extensive counsel is that they are experts in their fields, and you are not; you're an expert in the business arena. You would not expect a lawyer to come into your field of expertise and make the best and most profitable decisions, so you should not expect your abilities to carry you through the entire buying or selling process unless you are willing to accept that you will make costly mistakes and you won't achieve maximum profit.

This section of Chapter 2 will take a look at the potential members of your team and the assets they bring to the table. Since we have already discussed the role and responsibilities of the intermediary, we won't cover them again here. Just remember that the intermediary is also an important member of your team and will often interact with these members as much as or more than yourself.

Financiers

Financiers are very important persons for your advisory team. These individuals not only provide necessary information concerning financial options and capital funding, but they also tend to be able to recommend particular companies, financial institutions, or venture capitalists that may benefit your particular situation.

Business Valuation Expert

A business valuation expert is another valuable member since he or she must work very closely with your intermediary to establish the value of the potential business. Much of the entire process will be affected by the valuation process and the resulting monetary value assigned to the business. Negotiations sometimes hinge on the buy/sell price, and deals are made or broken depending upon the ability of the two parties to negotiate on price. The price is a derivative of the valuation placed on the business.

Equipment Appraiser

The machinery and equipment appraiser will work, for the most part, with your valuation expert. However, in some instances, when a large amount of the business value rests in the machinery and equipment, the merger-and-acquisition appraiser will actually work with both parties during the negotiation process, especially if there is some dispute as to the machinery and equipment valuations.

Real Estate Appraiser

A real estate appraiser will be needed if there is real estate involved in the business deal. Generally, small businesses are sold without the need for realty appraisal. Sometimes, however, a small business owner will choose to include the building and land as a part of the sale; in this case, you would need a real estate appraiser.

For the final members, your accountant and your lawyer, there are also some evaluation criteria you might want to use in making your selection. These two individuals will be two of the most important advisors you will retain; as such, they should meet certain qualifications and bring experience to the team.

Accountant

Accountants may be the first to know of potential businesses for sale, especially those in trouble. But that's only the beginning. Accountants can offer advice about buying and selling prices, how to assess a financial statement, and what the different financial ratios should be for a healthy business. There are some specific criteria your accountant should be able to meet in order to be of benefit as an experienced member of your team. A general guide to the criteria is as follows:

1. Are you familiar with acquisitions, and how many have you previously worked on?

2. Were you retained as the accountant after the acquisition?

3. Can you provide references?

4. What is your fee schedule?

5. Are you familiar with valuation methods used when determining business worth?

6. Can you successfully complete monthly financials necessary for due diligence?

7. Are you familiar with the tax elements involved in the sale or purchase of a business?

8. Will you personally handle the acquisition, or will one of your staff be assigned to the work?

Lawyer

A lawyer will always be a necessary member of any advisory team. Everything we do in today's business climate requires legal and binding agreements. Many times, the most costly mistakes we make are in entering into binding agreements that are not worded to our benefit. Often it's only after several months or years of operation that we begin to realize the error, and by then it's too late to get out of the agreement economically. Make sure that as you enter into a buy/sell agreement, you have had your attorney check and re-check the document and that any questionable wording is revised for clarity. The following are certain questions you would need an experienced and beneficial lawyer to answer:

1. Have you previously done any acquisitions work?

2. Were you retained as legal counsel for the business after the transaction?

3. Are you familiar with all aspects of the legalities involved in a Purchase Agreement?

4. Can you provide references?

5. What is your fee schedule?

6. Have you ever been involved in a lawsuit in reference to your work?

7. Will you personally handle the acquisition, or will one of your staff be assigned to the work?

KNOWING WHEN TO BUY OR SELL

Determining When to Buy

Matters to be considered include an understanding of your buyer and his or her motives, reputation of the business, objective of the seller, employee retention issues, potential for financing by owner, cash need of owner, cash flow of the business, length of time on the market, and the seller's next best option. Determining when to buy, from this standpoint, is the result of the first instinct and general knowledge you or your intermediary may have about a potential business. This particular section of Chapter 2 will not cover the detailed information that is covered in Chapters 4 and 5 concerning the financial and overall health of the business and the actual value of the business; these are the final determining factors once you've used this section as a general guide for tentative purchase intentions.

Owner burnout is one of the most common reasons small

businesses are placed on the market. The owner or founder has simply come to the place where there is no longer a desire to own and operate the business. In cases such as this, there is usually no difficulty in closing the deal once a reasonable buyout plan has been developed; there is very little concern for the company from an emotional standpoint, and the seller/owner is generally ready to leave.

If insufficient capital/no liquidity is the reason for selling, you may be buying a troubled business. Quite often, the business has come to the point that bankruptcy or solvency is the only other option. "Sick" companies are an easy target provided you have the access to turnaround specialists that can effectively bring the company back from the dead.

Adversity/divorce/illness will not be an issue for larger companies, but for small businesses, family situations such as terminal illness or divorce can bring about the need for tremendous change. Often, there is no other option available than to sell the business.

Many times, founders of small businesses love what they do; their children or relatives do not. Often, these small businesses are not run with the intention of ever being large businesses, so there is never a contingency plan when no family member is available or capable of continuing the family business. At that point, it is a somewhat forced sale, and this works to the buyer's advantage because many times the business is not in trouble. It is profitable and operating efficiently; there's just no captain available to steer the ship.

There are special situations that sometimes occur at just the right time and place. This is when the "perfect" deal exists. But for the vast majority of business buys and sells today, there is no perfect situation. The ability to recognize a diamond in the rough can often mean the difference between the profitable transaction and the transaction that never was. Seizing the moment is part instinct and part business knowledge and skill. If you understand the business and your advisory team does its job, finding a diamond in the rough is more technical than instinctual. If, however, you must act quickly in order to capitalize on a situation and there is no time for team review, it becomes a matter of instinct. If you are in your element, you are in a better position to trust your instincts; it's simply an extension of your business knowledge. There are three basic steps involved in achieving success: timing, vision, and action. These seem simple concepts, but bringing them all together into one particular, brief moment is often quite difficult. Not impossible, however.

If you have inside information or if you have knowledge that no one else has, you have opportunity; the where and the when are sometimes the missing elements. If you can combine the knowledge you have about a particular product or market with the opportunity to act, then you have a window of opportunity. Sometimes, that window is open only briefly. Your responsibility in evaluating your goals and objectives, performing self-assessments, and hiring intermediaries is to understand exactly what you're after and then act when opportunity presents itself.

Determining When to Sell

There are some key issues that should be addressed in determining when to sell your business, and your position as a business owner mandates that you examine those issues.

Determine if any of these situations apply to your business, and then act upon the knowledge you have. Let's take a moment to review those issues, and provide you with some basic information.

There are some very basic rules of thumb that can be used to determine when you should sell or buy a small business. The first is to be objective about the business; although small business owners are often quite compassionate about their employees and customers, no business is indispensable. Remaining objective and emotionally uninvolved will allow you to assess whether the time is right. Second, you need to consider selling a business if there is no heir apparent. If you have no apparent successor by the time you are nearing retirement age, then as a businessperson you should realize that it is time to seek either a competent CEO or sell. Third, sell when business is booming.

Everyone assumes that the best time to sell a cyclical or seasonal business is when it is at its peak; the same is true for all small businesses. As a founder, you have realized a dream. At this point; why not sell when your dream is thriving? As a buyer, the best time to come into a business is while it is on the upswing. Profits are generally high, and you often need some space and time to experience what is known as a "learning curve" or the opportunity to make mistakes and get to know your business boundaries. The best time for this is when you can best afford those mistakes.

Once you've determined that it's time to sell, what is the process for readying your business? The following paragraphs walk you through a step-by-step process that will enable you to position your business for selling at the best sale price. These steps should be taken at least one year prior to anticipating placing your business on the open market.

- **Step 1:** Consult with your CPA (presumably, you already have one either for your business needs or as a member of your advisory team). Begin to make any necessary tax-structure changes; in most situations, you will need to make this a dual consultation between your CPA and your legal counsel. Generally, there are also legal changes that need to be made simultaneously with tax-structure changes.

- **Step 2:** Do not make any capital improvements the year prior to placing the business for sale; you can use the cash better elsewhere. In addition, unless your equipment, fixtures, and buildings are in an extreme state of ill-repair, the new owners will not want to tie up large amounts of capital in new machinery, buildings, etc. You want to make the business as affordable as possible while reaping the most profit possible.

- **Step 3:** Make sure all the loose ends are tied and properly addressed. Loose ends usually pertain to establishing a market price and making sure you have time to review, research, and re-think your business price. This one factor alone can make or break deals. Be definite in your price criteria.

Just as a good résumé takes revision, so does a good selling memorandum. Working with your intermediary (who should typically have the literary skills), develop a selling memorandum that is a sure sell when it comes to promoting your business. After all, just like the résumé, this may be the only opportunity you have to present yourself or your business; make it good. The selling memorandum should contain much of the information that a business plan would: a detailed description of the company and products or services provided; its market segment and market share; financials; management team, and experience; the competitive edge; and its business strategy. A statement of your management strengths and weaknesses, evaluation of an adequate management force, and the level of importance the management plays in the success of your particular business should be available as a part of your selling memorandum.

Current financials through the current quarter and monthly financials should be made available as each month's end is complete. The financials must be accurate, honest, and spotless.

Non-compete employee contracts, consulting contracts, and vendor contracts (that is, written contracts with vendors, suppliers, customers, etc.) that would affect a prospective buyer should be a part of the package.

Make sure that your business environment is as up to date as possible; make sure that all areas are clean and reasonably kept.

Knowing when to sell is a combination of the above issues as well as pure instinct and intuition. Learning to trust your gut feeling when you're in business for yourself is something you will need to develop. For those already in business, trusting this feeling is often the difference between a success and failure. It's also a very useful tool when evaluating potential buyers.

There are certainly separate, very distinct phases that a buyer or seller will move through during the course of the buying, owning, and selling process. You are, at this point, still in the beginning steps for the buy-and-sell proposition. It may seem that the process described here increases the time it will take to place your business on the market or for the buyer to locate a potential business to buy. In some areas it does take longer to accomplish your objective. But in the end, and as you come to the close of the journey, you will reap the benefit, usually monetarily, from having properly prepared yourself and the business. As you complete this chapter, you have accomplished a great deal toward your primary objective. Let's take just a moment to review.

At this point, as a buyer or seller, you have laid the following groundwork and completed the following tasks:

1. You understand your profile as a buyer or seller.

2. You have a clear understanding of the type of business you're buying or selling.

3. You've established the search criteria whether you're searching for a buyer or locating a business.

4. You've developed the search plan.

5. You've established the responsibilities you expect your intermediary to assume.

6. You've developed the search criteria for locating an intermediary.

7. You've located and hired an intermediary.

8. You've located and put into place an acquisition team or a team of advisors for selling your business.

When you stop to look at your list of accomplishments, it is easy to see how this process can consume more than six months of your time; as you take the time to properly address your desires, expectations, and process boundaries, you are also taking a major step toward the realization of your dream.

CASE STUDY

Tenn Tom 1 Stop, Inc. is a family-owned-and-operated business that caters to the convenience store retail sales market. This case study is exceptionally special, as this owner happens to be the mentor/parent for the author of the book, *How to Buy and/or Sell a Small Business for Maximum Profit.* Businesses like this have been a lifetime commitment for the owner, Harry Vice.

Contact Information: Harry T. Vice
13997 Hwy 388
Brooksville, MS 39739

I became a business owner because it was a lifelong dream. I announced in the third grade in school that I wanted to own and operate a store, and I made the dream come true. When I started Tenn Tom 1 Stop, Inc., I thought it was the perfect marriage of my desire to meet people and to fulfill my dream of business ownership.

Owning a business has been a way to keep my mental capacities sharp; business ownership demands that you stay on top of an ever-changing environment, and if you succeed, you must be aware of the constant changes. It's been extremely satisfying at the end of the day, to sit back and realize that although you're extremely tired, you're building something that belongs to you.

I also brought to the business a good work ethic, excellent knowledge of people, enjoyment of the retail sales environment, an attitude of willingness, and information about the industry in relation to community needs.

With hard work and commitment, business ownership has provided me with a means to provide substantially well for my family, to live well in a time and place that didn't necessarily provide that opportunity for everyone around me in the community.

Any disadvantage to be found is that you must dedicate the bulk of your time toward succeeding in business; it leaves very little time to be at home in charge of child-rearing and companionship with a spouse. Furthermore, there's no retirement plan; you're at the mercy of your success. You must overcome the mindset of the masses. There is no guarantee; it is a gamble in the sense that you're not guaranteed a successful outcome.

I feel as though I've added to the economic value

of the community. I provided jobs in an economically depressed area. I provided through donations to the community, and through providing necessary services in an area that would otherwise not had them available.

To date, I've sold three businesses for the profit and because it was time to move on. To determine the value of each business, I used a combination of valuation methods. Goodwill certainly added to the value of my businesses. I financed the sale of my business with a seller-financed mortgage. In my case, because I held a mortgage on the physical property, I could have recouped any unpaid mortgage.

I provided the buyer with general information about the business. At the time of the sale, the businesses I sold were not actively marketed. I was approached about selling by each buyer that actually closed the deal. No lawyers or attorneys were used; each time I sold a business, my accountant and the local bank provided any legal services or contracts I needed. Furthermore, my accountant advised me as to the best choices concerning capital gains, and I walked away with as much tax exemption as possible.

I would say that owning a small business is an occupation a person must feel like he is ready to try, to seize the moment; you need to look within yourself and know if you're ready, because it's going to take extreme commitment, planning, patience, and a strong desire to succeed to attain profitability in a small business.

CHAPTER 3

THE STRATEGIES

Key issues covered in this chapter are:

- *Marketing Strategies for Buying and Selling*
- *Selling Strategies*
- *Identifying a Buyer*
- *Value Drivers*
- *Sell, Sell, Sell*
- *Buying Strategies*
- *Understanding the Seller*

MARKETING STRATEGIES FOR BUYING OR SELLING

Selling Strategies

The strategy that works for your situation may be any one of the following, or it may be a combination of them. The key here is to find the strategy that best fits you, your search criteria, and the industry you will search within. Some of the strategies we will discuss achieve great results in a particular industry but are absolutely not conducive to other industries. Work with your intermediary and your team of advisors to determine which strategy best suits your individual situation.

Horse-Race Approach

This approach is virtually self-explanatory in nature. There are certain conditions that might indicate that a seller should choose this approach. The key is an understanding of the seller and the seller's objectives. Quite often, individuals will place their businesses for sale due to the burnout effect; when this occurs, sellers often are just eager to get out of the situation. Opportunities of this nature place the edge on the side of the buyer for no good reason. The company isn't in trouble, the owners aren't in any sort of financial or medical emergency; they're just simply tired of doing what they've been doing. When this approach to marketing is used, the seller foregoes the typical process of readying the company for sale and may often completely skip the professional business valuation, preferring to simply ask a price that will be likely to bring an immediate buy proposal and move on with the sale. Is this the best approach under these conditions? Absolutely not; however, as a buyer, I certainly would capitalize on such an opportunity.

The other condition that is often present when this approach is used (this is generally what 85 percent of horse-race strategies will fall within) is trouble in the company. While this is not the only approach that may be used, it is often the only option remaining once the seller realizes that the business must be sold. In buying and selling small businesses, quite often small business owners will not see that the end is in sight. Even if they do possibly see that disaster is imminent, they will not sell or consider selling until there is absolutely no other alternative. At this point, immediate sale is the best option and may be the only alternative to a complete shutdown of the business. Even under the immediacy of the horse-race approach, it will usually be several months before a target buyer can be found. Under certain conditions, the business may or may not be able to continue operations.

Partner with Professionals

In my opinion, this is the best marketing strategy. Hire a professional marketing team to package and prepare your business for sale. Or, as so many individuals do, hire a team of assistants that can and will assist you in marketing your business. Either way, you have the advantage of working with professionals that can and will place your business in the best light possible. Just as you would not expect a person without experience in business to step in and operate it as successfully as a seasoned businessperson, you cannot expect to step into the shoes of a professional marketing agent or the various professionals you could retain to help you package your business and successfully accomplish what they have spent years perfecting. Sometimes the best marketing strategy is simply understanding when to let professionals do their jobs.

Non-Compete Agreements

This marketing strategy is used in situations where the business is thriving but the threat of competition from the existing owner would prohibit the sale of the business; in such cases, the inclusion of a non-compete agreement as a part of the marketing information and selling memorandum provides an inducement for a possible buyer. These marketing strategies are most often used in service industries or small service businesses that are for sale.

Once you've determined which strategy you will use, you can then move into determining the remaining marketing strategy criteria such as identifying the buyers that fit the strategy you are employing and the value drivers within the business that make the business an appealing sell. Then you are ready to present the business as best you can with the selling memorandum.

Identify the Buyer

As you enter this phase of the process, the target buyer can be quite elusive, and you can never have too many sources for the location of a potential buyer. This section will provide you with insight and ideas for your own strategy in establishing a target buyer and perhaps impart some knowledge about the process and criteria you had not previously considered.

The most important knowledge you can have going into this process is simply knowing buyer types: strategic, competitive, financial, international, customer/vendor, and individual. These buyer types purchase businesses for different reasons and with different objectives in mind; understanding which particular type you're dealing with will provide you with an edge during the negotiations or even during the valuation of your business. Let's take a moment to define and evaluate each type.

The Strategic Buyer

This is an individual or group of individuals who will purchase a business as a complement to an already existing business. It is much more profitable and transitions can be made much more easily if you purchase a business that is in a related field. The new owners can often tie together the existing and new business into a more profitable one and reap immediate benefits in both areas.

The Competitive Buyer

This buyer is one who purchases a business that is in competition with his own. The advantage in purchasing as a competitive buyer is that often the existing business can merge with the new business to offer cost advantages, increase market share, and reduce expenses. Quite often mergers of competitive companies will occur for the benefit of both companies. They are not usually direct competitors; in other words, they sell to the same customers, but they are not competitors in the same field. Sometimes the high-end business will merge with the low-end business; for example: Sears and Kmart. Both are retail sales competitors; Sears, however, has a high-end market while Kmart markets to the cheaper, lower end. The two businesses combined corner a larger market share.

The Financial Buyer

This buyer purchases businesses for investment. This buyer will use financial engineering to increase the profitability of the company either through additional acquisitions that make the company more valuable or through management and personnel changes that increase profitability. Quite often, there have been prior acquisitions or planned additional acquisitions that serve to enhance the appeal and profitability of the business. The financial buyer usually only retains a business for five to seven years, increases profitability and value, and then returns the business or businesses to the selling market.

International Buyers

These are the crème de la crème of the buyers' market. They are often absentee owners who pay a premium price to acquire a business, especially if the business has excellent channels of distribution in the United States. Currently, there has been a surge in this type of buyer in China, as the economy there continues to grow at an astonishing pace.

The Customer or Vendor Buyer

This buyer utilizes the vertical-integration approach, which has been used recently with some success. Often, in the buy/sell market, using the vertical-integration approach can prove too difficult a transition, or the expertise required to complete the process proves too costly. Additionally, the training in one is not easily transferred nor is it useful in another.

The Individual Buyer

The most common type, this buyer should be well-qualified, experienced, and have the financial backing or capital required for the purchase. Some readers might question why you would care if the individual buyer is qualified and experienced: You are selling the business, so you should have no further concern with the operations. But this is not true. Should you sell to an individual who is poorly qualified or lacking in experience and the business fails, you run the risk of being sued for misrepresentation of the business.

Especially in buyout situations, competitors or customers are excellent potential buyers. These are the businesses and individuals most likely to have an interest in your success or failure; therefore, they often will show interest when presented with the opportunity to acquire a complementary business. This is an extension of the strategic or competitive buyer; if you prepare wisely and research industry information, you can generally produce several potential buyers in this category worth targeting.

Are there other methods that can be used to target buyers?

Absolutely. There are some good places you can begin a search other than within your own industry. Trade shows, trade publications, networking, and associations such as those made up of investment bankers, merger and acquisition specialists, and corporate finance associates are excellent sources, just to name a few.

In an earlier paragraph, we mentioned that you should select individuals or companies that would perceive your business as valuable. What are some of those value drivers? Let's take a moment to evaluate value drivers and what you as a seller (or buyer) should look for.

Value Drivers

Understanding what makes a business valuable goes a long way in your preparation and pursuit of a buyer. There can be many unique and inexplicable reasons behind the valuation of a particular industry or business; however, for this book and in order to impart a general understanding, we will examine the most common value drivers and to what extent they affect your business valuation.

History of the business, the industry, and competition; the products and services offered; the customers and marketing program; the suppliers, operations, and facilities; the current management structure; and the legal and tax implications of a sale are the broad-based value drivers in any business and, as such, deserve some exploration and discussion here.

The history of a business can give you tremendous insight as to the past operations and problems of the business; sometimes the problems have a way of lingering and remaining problems even after the sale of a business.

Industry and competition refers to the process of evaluating the internal operations of the business and the external influences of the industry as they apply to the business. There are entire books that focus primarily on the external forces that affect a business; the simple conclusion we need to reach in examining these internal and external influences is that the greater our understanding of these forces, the better we can identify areas that can potentially alter the competitive environment and thus the operations of the business. Key points to consider when evaluating the industry and competition values include the following:

1. Is the industry regional or national?

2. Is the industry expanding or contracting?

3. Is there foreign competition? To what extent does competition affect operations?

4. Are there external factors in the immediate future (3–5 years) that might affect the industry (legislation, technology, environmental issues)?

5. What is the principal competitive edge (price, service, location)?

6. Are there barriers to competing profitably?

7. Are there available resources that will be required to gain the competitive edge?

8. Are there any signs of competitor mergers? Market domination?

You may find these questions are sufficient to perform the evaluation, or you may find that there is a need to include or exclude certain questions; that's perfectly acceptable since the objective here is to evaluate your particular situation, so tailor the questions to meet your evaluation needs.

I believe products and services are among the most important value drivers. The core products and services of the business are the heart of the business. Just like human beings, businesses must have their hearts to function and thrive. Understanding the key products or services offered by a business provides you with the insight you need to develop the evaluation criteria. Fundamental questions you should ask:

1. What are the principal products and/or services?

2. How diversified is the business?

3. What are the most competitive products or services?

4. What is the selling history of the business?

5. Are there any proprietary products such as patents, trademarks, etc.?

6. Are there any impending technological changes that would affect the product or service and its ability to compete?

7. Are there any liabilities associated with the products or services?

8. What types of warranties exist, and are there any outstanding product problems?

9. Are there any protected territory issues?

10. Does the business produce any substitute or

complementary products?

During your evaluation of these value drivers, you are also developing an understanding of the revenue-generating products or services and the loopholes or opportunities for capitalizing on potential revenues that exist. This brings us to the next value driver: consumers and marketing.

Consumers and marketing value drivers refer to the basic belief that the purpose of a business is to create and keep customers. Identification of the target market, the marketing strategy in place, and any untapped markets provide the potential buyer the information needed to see opportunities not yet taken. The following questions are meant to serve as a general guide and should aid you in your valuation.

- Are the customers individuals or businesses?

- What is the target market?

- Do you have an excellent understanding of your customers' purchasing process?

- Are there any government customers?

- Are there problems with aging accounts, credit ratings, etc.?

- Are any of the existing customers in a troubled or failing industry?

- Is the customer base growing, declining, or stagnant?

- What percentage of the revenue do the top ten customers account for?

- Is the business primarily reliant on just a handful or one customer?

- Are there any existing maintenance or sales agreements?

- Is the product or service need-based or dispensable?

- Has the business been effective in reaching the target market?

- What is the current advertising campaign?

- Is there more than one target market?

- What media are used to deliver products to market?

- Are there any current or anticipated market changes that would affect business revenue?

- Are there any potential untapped markets?

In completing the evaluation of these value drivers, you need to understand that consumers and marketing may be the most important value drivers and will definitely deserve your full attention.

Suppliers, operations, and facilities are distinctly separate but heavily reliant on each other in creating a successful and profitable product or service offering. Suppliers can have a tremendous effect on the profitability levels and the ability of the business to meet contract deadlines. Pointed questions to ask in looking at these value drivers are the following:

1. How many suppliers are there?

2. Have any of the suppliers experienced financial difficulties?

3. Does any one supplier account for more than 10 percent of the business's raw material needs?

4. What are the payment terms with suppliers?

5. Are the business relationships with suppliers good?

6. Are there any outstanding contractual obligations with suppliers?

The combination of supplier value and operations and facilities issues all come together in the overall process of completing the product or providing the service and are for this reason covered together here. Once you've evaluated the supplier issues, you are in a position to move right into the operations and facilities concerns. Key questions at this juncture are as follows:

1. Are the facilities neat, clean, and modern?

2. What is the size of the facility? Is the facility operating at capacity?

3. Does the business own or lease the equipment? How is it serviced?

4. Is the equipment properly maintained and current for industry standards?

5. Is there a strategic plan in place?

6. Is there a quality control program in place?

7. How is the facility managed?

8. Does the business own or lease the facility?

9. Can the business be moved?

10. Is there adequate space for increased production?

11. Does the business meet or exceed production/service-delivery deadlines?

If the business facility (equipment and building) are to play a significant role in the financial valuation of the business, a thorough and diligent evaluation of this area will reveal not only the depth of the value of the facility to the business as a part of the operation, but also the monetary value of the facility and equipment.

The current management structure evaluation can reveal many things about where a business, even one that is profitable and meets the due-diligence requirements for financial assessment, is headed. There have been many, many business failures that could be tied directly to a lack of proper management. Understanding the strengths and weaknesses of your management structure and current management team is a key factor in developing a proper assessment of the business value. You need to ask the following questions:

1. What is the organizational structure of the business?

2. Who currently handles the day-to-day operations?

3. To what extent does the current owner control decisions about finance? marketing? operations?

4. Are there any specialized managers?

5. What is the relationship between the current

management team and the owner?

6. Do you intend to be an absentee owner?

7. What are your strengths and weaknesses, and does current management complement those?

8. Have there been any employee-related lawsuits?

9. How well do you fit with current management?

Answering these questions not only helps you understand current management issues, it helps you understand your position and fit should the business be purchased. Making a proper assessment of the value you bring to the business is as important as assessing the value of the managers retained and the potential buyer.

The legal and tax implications of the sale, although not as obvious, can add or detract tremendously as an element of value to the business. Often, when individuals or partnerships are formed, there are legal issues that are never properly addressed. When the time comes to sell the business, there are issues that can prove costly to the buyer and the seller. As part of the due-diligence process, these questions may be addressed again, but in determining accurate value, ask the following questions:

- Are there any outstanding judgments against the individual, the partners, or the business?

- Are there any current transferable contract obligations between the business, suppliers, vendors, and/or employees?

- Are there any government regulations, tax codes, or

environmental requirements previously violated that are still pending action?

- Are there any pending lawsuits or any previously settled for which the business is liable?

- Are there any non-compete covenants or agreements between the business and any other individuals, businesses, or legal entities?

Basic questions and answers about the legal and tax responsibilities of the business must be answered before you can accurately place a value on the business.

This brings us to the end of the usual and customary value drivers that are used during the valuation of a business. This does not mean that the above-listed examples are a perfect fit for your situation; it does, however, give you a general idea of how to proceed and the basic style of questioning that should be used to value the business. This discussion of value drivers is included in this section for the seller (although it would appear it is a buyer's format) simply because a seller must approach the valuation from both perspectives; when a buyer enters into the process, you must be prepared to answer these types of questions. Omitting any important piece of information from a selling memorandum or discussions with prospective buyers is sometimes an irreversible mistake.

The last and tremendously subjective topic covered under marketing strategy is your ability to sell yourself, your business, and the potential or future value of the business. Remember that sellers sell the past, and buyers buy the future. The packaging and presentation often spell success or failure as the past passes to the future.

Sell, Sell, Sell

You can't sell a product successfully if you don't believe in the product. Who better than you, the owner, to sell your company? To a very great extent you are the best candidate as far as your ability to represent your business during the buy/sell process. Once you have the intermediary, the selling memorandum, and a potential buyer, your ability to enthusiastically sell yourself and your business is a key to the acceptance of a proposal. The following paragraphs will address your role as the business owner in packaging and selling your business.

Represent your company enthusiastically. You're selling a business that will require work, dedication, and commitment from the buyer; in other words, your sale is going to require that the buyer meet additional obligations and responsibilities, which makes it more difficult. In general, the more inspired and passionate you are as a seller, the more receptive the buyer (potentially) is to the selling proposition.

Package your company well in the selling memorandum. The selling memorandum is often the first impression a potential buyer has of your business. First impressions are sometimes the only opportunity you get to pitch your business. Make every effort possible to produce an effective and eloquent representation. More attention to this detail is given during Chapter 9: The Deal; the steps involved in a successful negotiation can be found there.

Use an intermediary to bolster the company's image. Sometimes, the intermediary is an invaluable source of information to the seller when putting together effective proposals. During the initial stages of procuring a buyer, a third-party opinion, even if it is a compensated opinion, goes a long way in swaying potential buyers.

Be upfront with contract obligations, pending legal action, lease obligations, or prepayment deposits from customers. The fastest way to lose a potential buyer is to withhold or conceal negative information. Once the due diligence has been undertaken, most information, good or bad, has been detected, reviewed, and discussed between the buyer, seller, and intermediaries. Your best option, and the best advice that anyone can follow, is to be honest and upfront and never fail to present any negative information in the most advantageous light. Be truthful, but also use the opportunity to its fullest potential.

Buying Strategies

You can negotiate a buy or sell proposition and never fully understand some of the key issues that prompted the sale, but if you want to negotiate the best deal possible, you need to understand some of the basic strategies for accomplishing that purpose. In the paragraphs below, we're going to discuss some of the more successful strategies used today to make a good buy even better. This information was covered briefly in Chapter 2; the information is presented here as an in-depth look at the strategies you develop as a buyer based on the reasons the seller may have for placing the business for sale. The information is covered more extensively here and from an entirely different point of view. The key points discussed here include understanding the seller, incorporating flexibility into your buying terms, having a clear understanding of the different forms of business organization, retaining current management, and performing due diligence in the strategic acquisition of a business. As always, the services of an intermediary in establishing the strategy to be used and in carrying out the key points of your strategic plan are of extreme value to all parties—buyers and sellers. As a buyer, however, retaining an intermediary to aid in the execution of the chosen strategy makes for a better chance of success. Often, during negotiations and in the process of utilizing the strategy you've developed, an intermediary is able to objectively accomplish the task at hand; highly involved buyers allow emotions to rule at times. Quite often, strategy success will depend upon nerves and patience. As the buyer, you will be short on both.

Understanding the Seller

When you take the time to understand your seller, you are making an investment in your future: the ownership of a business. Generally, if you intend to invest several hundred thousand dollars or perhaps even a couple of million dollars, you would be remiss if you did not spend some time investigating the business and the business owners. In Chapter 2 we discussed the possible reasons why a business was placed on the market; here we are going to discuss these reasons from the strategic standpoint of the buyer's gaining an understanding of the seller and the position a buyer can take once he or she has gained an in-depth understanding of the seller.

The first question you should ask as a buyer is, Why is the business really for sale? What are the owner's real goals? Often, the response of "the business is growing too rapidly for the current owner to keep pace" is simply not the complete truth. If you choose, you can accept that at face value, but be warned that this occurs in only a small minority of selling situations. The vast majority of businesses are sold for these reasons: no heir available, burnout, the business has lost the competitive edge either through asset depletion or market share, the original owner has passed and the estate cannot afford to keep the business, or there has been an offer to buy that is simply too good to refuse.

If you have investigated your seller and the business and have found that the business is indeed operating at peak performance in a growing and profitable industry, then your strategic approach lies in understanding the importance of the business to the seller and promoting yourself as the best candidate for acquisition of the business. This particular reason for selling a business places the seller in the most favorable light possible: He or she is in possession of a growing and profitable business with no urgent need or desire to sell. If the seller is selling simply because the offer to buy has been too good to refuse, obviously the buyer has not read this book and has more money than good common sense. I don't believe there's the need for a strategic approach here.

Now that we've covered the less desirable conditions from the buyer's standpoint, let's take a look at the favorable conditions for buying and the most successful strategic approach. Should the seller choose to sell for any of the other reasons (no heir available, the business has lost the competitive edge, the original owner has passed and the estate cannot afford to retain the business, or the business is in other financial trouble), the buyer has the edge and can make use of a strategy known as leveraging. You have leveraging power if the seller needs to sell. You can dictate some degree of the buy/sell terms and certainly the negotiated price. Time is generally not on the side of the seller, so you have another leveraging tool. This information concerning strategic positioning will not be available to you if you do not take the time to investigate the company and the seller. I will repeat once again: You cannot place a price on the invaluable process of due diligence.

There is an additional aspect of understanding your seller that we haven't touched on: why sellers don't sell. Your position as the buyer and the strategy that you use will rely in part on the pieces of information about your seller that would prohibit or delay the negotiation and selling process. There are reasons that a seller will refuse the offer: a seller is asking too much for the business (at which point you should withdraw from negotiations and cut your losses); there are capital-gains and tax issues (these items are addressed in depth in Chapters 8 and 9); or the owner has lost salary (this issue also will be addressed in detail in Chapter 9). There are avenues for addressing these issues other than an asking price that exceeds the valuation that allow the buyer and seller to come to an agreement with just a little negotiation of the finer points and some flexibility on behalf of both parties.

Remember, capitalize on the real issues for the seller and negotiate the finer points; in other words, pick your battles when dealing and negotiating. This brings us now to the next key issue: flexibility.

Be flexible with your buying terms. Just as you must compromise in a relationship, you must compromise during the course of the buy/sell process and especially during the negotiations; after all, that's the purpose of the negotiations. As a buyer, you may need the seller to assume some of the financing with a seller-financed mortgage or with earn-out options. You need to be willing to give as well. An extensive discussion of flexibility and the negotiation process will be covered in Chapter 9: The Deal. We mention it here simply for the purpose of clarifying the need for flexibility in your strategy formula as a buyer.

Understand the value of business organization (S corporation versus C corporation), management retention, and due diligence. A complete understanding of the organizational structure of the business you intend to buy will give you access to information that can be used to formulate a buyout strategy that will work in your favor and hopefully the seller's favor upon closing the deal and disbursing funds. This understanding of business organization will also give you a clearer picture of your liabilities and tax rates once you acquire the business should you choose to leave the organizational structure as is. If the business would better benefit you in another form, you need to make those changes during the negotiating of the deal and the closing process.

Retaining the current management and even, in some circumstances, the current owners for a specific period of time can often prove to be a useful leveraging tool during the establishment of a buying strategy. Many owners of small businesses feel a loyalty to their employees, especially management, that would encourage the sale if management were going to be retained. This tactic not only enhances the negotiations, but it is also a true benefit to the incoming buyer in many situations; retaining members of management can help to ensure a smooth transition. This, too, is discussed in greater detail in Chapter 10: The Transition.

During the investigation of the business and the business's history and in developing an understanding of the seller, you are performing the non-financial aspect of due diligence. The importance of due diligence, from a financial standpoint and from a non-financial standpoint, cannot be measured. Often, when due diligence has been successfully and properly performed, you as a buyer will discover more valuable information than you might need but never more than you can use. Every piece of information and all the knowledge you can acquire about a business places you closer to successfully implementing the most beneficial strategy and closing the deal at the most beneficial price.

CASE STUDY

Country Scents is a small, family-owned-and-operated candle-making business that came into existence as a result of a family crisis; the business provided not only the necessary income for living expenses, but also a way for the family to cope with illness. Country Scents continues today to work with local charities and fundraising events through donations of their sales and time to further many forms of medical research.

Contact Information: Pam Cooper
470 Margaret St./P.O. Box 261
Millport, AL 35576

In May of 1999, at the age of 38, my husband had a stroke, and we discovered the he also had a heart defect. With two young children at home, and regular household and medical expenses, we had to find a way for us to produce a regular income. The candle business was my husband's idea; he had the idea for candle making long before it became a reality. After the stroke and surgery, he needed something creative, and I needed work. We merged the two needs with his earlier idea of candle making, and it became Country Scents. We have succeeded because of a love of candles, a creative ability, and the determination to make it work.

We operate as a sole proprietorship and only had need of a business license and name reservation in order to operate; we handled those requirements ourselves.

Owning a small business has allowed me to be my own boss, to be available when Gary needs my attention, and it has given us a common ground and a creative outlet as a couple. Additionally, the business helped us financially to make it through the early years after the stroke, and to keep our family and home intact.

Owning and operating a business is time consuming, and you have to learn to separate your business life from your personal life, and make time for both. It is a 24/7 responsibility. The tremendous responsibility that is a part of operating a business is in areas of finance, making ends meet, profitability, etc. All of these issues must be dealt with by only a couple of people in small family-owned businesses.

Having candles (and small gifts) brings tremendous joy and happiness to our customers; when you make and sell these items, you get to see firsthand the

affect your business can have on the people in the community.

I would recommend small business ownership, but a lot of it would depend upon the individual. It's been a great way for us to live: my husband could find some therapy with the creativity involved in putting together marketing and new product ideas. I was able to fill the shoes I needed to fill and be available for my family; it's been my recreation and my escape as well as a way to help make a living.

PART II:

THE
JOURNEY

CHAPTER 4

THE EVALUATION

Key issues covered in this chapter are:

- *Due Diligence*
- *Evaluating the Overall Health of a Business*
- *Evaluating the Financial Health of a Business*
- *Financial Analysis*
- *Ratios*
- *Sensitivity and Break-Even Analysis*

DUE DILIGENCE

Due diligence as a part of the evaluation process must be no less than perfect. Due diligence is performed on the non-financial, financial, and legal records of the business in order to verify that the information that has been furnished is accurate. Quite frankly, this is the most important phase of the entire process. You can make mistakes, become lax in your endeavor, and even ignore advice that you're given by professionals, but you must not be remiss in your due-diligence efforts. Every aspect of your future and the business's future will rely on the accurate verification of information. Careful planning and expert advice will ensure successful due-diligence proceedings. The

information you will need to complete the due-diligence process
is covered extensively in this chapter; however, it is during
the deal structuring and negotiation process that you will take
the information discussed in this chapter and put together an
agreement that includes all pertinent pieces of information.
It will either protect you or leave you exposed at the end of
the negotiations. Both parties must be acutely aware of the
importance of the due-diligence process. The three basic areas of
due diligence are financial, legal, and business. An explanation
of each follows as well as instructions for performing each one.
Business and legal due diligence are covered simultaneously
in the section "Establishing the Overall Health of a Business";
Financial due diligence is explained and examined in the section
"Evaluating the Overall Financial Health of a Business."

Business due diligence examines the products; the market; the
surrounding economic conditions, if applicable; competitors;
legislation that could affect the business; and any expected
industry changes that could impact the profitability of the
business. In essence, you can never know too much about a
business; it is here where general knowledge of the business
arena you're entering and a network of associates that can give
you inside information about any upcoming industry or market
changes are so valuable.

Legal due diligence investigates territorial information, status
of contracts, any existing legal liabilities, any pending legal
liabilities, contract services, and lease and equipment purchase
conditions. In addition, you should also look at any legal
repercussions, such as binding contracts with suppliers that lock
the company into certain buying levels or price structures.

Financial due diligence refers to an intensive examination of the business books; sales, cost of goods, and labor are only minor pieces of the puzzle. One method that often reveals discrepancies in accounting figures is to compare the tax returns to the actual financial statements; if there are huge differences in numbers there, you need to dig deeper. If everything checks out, move on to the accounts receivables, payables, and inventory. Are there any "dead" accounts? Is there any obsolete inventory listed on the asset sheet? Look also at expenses; are there any major industry changes that would affect the expenses associated with operating the business? All of this information is useful as you prepare to go to the negotiation table. Any discrepancies can be used to negotiate a reduced selling price.

Evaluating the Overall Health of a Business

How do you evaluate the health of a business? Believe it or not, there are vital signs for a business just as there are vital signs for people. Understanding what to look for, how to look, and where to look will make your evaluation process much easier; and sometimes the results will surprise you. An evaluation of the non-financial information can reveal as much about the state of the business as the financials.

Market share refers to the primary market or target audience for the business. During the initial evaluation, establishing this rudimentary piece of information will often provide insight about the immediate future of the business or the industry to which the business markets its products. If the market share is shrinking for reasons other than those that are directly related to business operations, you might want to re-think your decision.

Economic factors will contribute tremendously to profitability; if you're working in a recessive economy, it's going to be twice as hard to market your product and meet cash flow obligations.

On a smaller scale, if your market is a local one, any influences on the local economy can drastically affect your sales dollars.

Growth opportunities will become apparent or non-apparent as you begin to examine the economic factors that influence the business. If the business is in an industry poised for exponential growth, there will more than likely also be additional growth opportunity either in obtaining a bigger market share through joint ventures or expansion of services and/or products offered.

Marketability is highly reliant upon market share, economics, and growth opportunities, which is why it follows those three in the order of our discussion. Product or services marketability will be partially determined by those outside influences listed above, and partially upon your ability to "sell" yourself or your product or service. You should have a much better understanding of yourself by now, and if you take the time to evaluate the outside influences, you should be able, through deductive reasoning, to assess the marketability of the business with the addition of your leadership. There will, however, be one more additional area of influence: management.

Management should be examined carefully. What is the current scope of management, what role does it play in the day-to-day operations, and how would this change after the buy/sell arrangement? Key personnel and effective, knowledgeable managers can often mean the difference between successful beginnings and rocky ones. You will want to ascertain who will stay and who will go; this will provide you with greater insight as to your immediate needs and whether or not you will need to recruit new management prior to the transition into new ownership.

Know the history of the company you're buying. When was it founded? Are you dealing with the original owner? Has the business operated continuously? These are a minimum of questions that should be answered prior to negotiating for the purchase of a business. The benefit is not purely for the purpose of establishing a business valuation, however; it can often give a buyer the edge when negotiating purchase price and terms with the seller.

1. When was the business started?

2. What product or service does the business provide?

3. Has this always been the basis of operations for the business?

4. Was the current owner the original owner?

5. How long has the current owner participated in this business? in this industry?

6. Has the company operated continuously over the life of the company?

7. Has the business been involved in any legal issues such as bankruptcy, lawsuits, or tax liens?

Know the industry the business is involved in and have a very good understanding of the state of the industry. For instance, during the 1980s as the steel industry began to decline, it would not have been a great time to purchase a steel mill; not unless you intended to move it to another country! Investing the amount of time necessary to understand the outside forces that will affect your business is as important as the time it takes to evaluate the internal forces. All of the factors will come together to create the environment, economics, and operating conditions that you will deal with for the next several years. You owe it to yourself to understand all aspects before coming to the negotiating table.

1. What is the average size of a company within the industry this business operates?

2. Is the industry expanding or shrinking?

3. What external factors might influence the industry in the future, such as legislation, technology, etc.?

4. Does foreign competition influence the industry?

5. Is the industry national or regional?

6. Is the industry dominated by market giants, or are there many small competitors?

7. Is there an industry leader?

Competitive environment refers to current competition, emerging competition, and the competitive nature of the business you're purchasing or selling. Quite often, small businesses are concerned only with the local environment and economy. Is the business a viable, healthy competitor under current operating conditions? Make sure there are no hidden factors such as anticipated economic upheaval or tremendous improvements in a competitor product or service that would prompt the current owner to put the business on the market. Sometimes, there is an underlying reason for a decision to sell. Take the necessary time to evaluate the economic climate that you will need to operate within, and gain as much knowledge as possible about any local competition. Any knowledge of the business gained during the initial evaluation will be of tremendous benefit to you now and in the later phases of actual operation.

1. How many firms are direct competitors?

2. How is the competition manifested in the workplace (price, new products, etc.)?

3. Which of these strategies is employed by the industry leader?

4. What is the principal base of competitive advantage?

5. What resources are necessary to participate in this competition (capital, creative prowess, salesmanship, etc.)?

6. Are there any signs of collusion or cooperation among firms in the industry?

7. What barriers to entry exist?

8. What barriers to exit exist?

This particular aspect of the evaluation should merit much of your time, even more than the financial information. Why? Because if there are going to be some major changes in the economic environment, competitor products, or even legislation that drastically increases your liability, expenditures, or production process, you're going to be severely crippled in your ability to operate profitably. Make sure that you devote ample time not only to the company but to the operating environment, the industry, and the legal issues surrounding the business.

Product and/or service examination should also be a part of your overall evaluation. Make sure the business is not in the declining years of its existence. The best time to purchase or sell a business is during its peak simply due to the fact that the business is worth more during peak operation. If you are a new owner, coming in to a business during the peak years of operation provides you with the extra cash needed to keep the business profitable while you have the opportunity to put a fresh face on the product or service.

1. What is the principal product or service?

2. How many services does the company offer or how many products does the company produce?

3. What are the competing products or services on the market?

4. How do they compare with this company's products or services?

5. What is the sales volume of the competitive product?

6. Are product or service sales seasonal?

7. How complex is the product or service?

8. Does the company have any proprietary products such as patents, trademarks, copyrights, or trade secrets?

9. Are there any apparent liabilities associated with the product or service?

10. Are there any fundamental technological or legislative changes about to take place that will significantly affect

the way the product or service is made or delivered?

11. Are there viable substitutes?

12. What is the history of the product or service within the business and from competitors?

As you examine the products or services of the business, you are going to want to pay particular attention to the product liability history, the market to whom the product is sold, and any liability activity within this market. If you've never heard of express warranties or implied warranties, now would be a good time for you to become familiar with these terms and understand what they mean in relation to the product or service of the business you're proposing to purchase. Many companies have been ruined financially and crippled to the point of bankruptcy because of liability and tort rulings that mandated payment of excessive fines and/or damages because of product liability cases.

Consumers and marketing will play a tremendous role in the continued success of the business. As you evaluate the current information available about the business, take a moment to examine the customer base and the marketing strategies and techniques used by the current owner. Is the maximum base being reached? Is a particular minority market segment the primary target, or is the consumer and marketing program being maximized? Examination of the consumer and marketing program in place will give you an excellent idea about your possibility for expanding on the existing opportunity or the need to create a new market. As a seller, this can also be a selling point; if you're not currently reaching a broad consumer base and you can illustrate to a potential buyer that the marketing program is not reaching an already existing consumer, you have a ready-made intangible asset to add to the value of the business. Let's first take a look at the questions you will want to ask concerning the consumer base:

1. Who are the primary customers of the business?

2. Are they individual or industrial consumers?

3. What are the demographics of the target market, assuming most customers are individuals?

4. If most of your customers are industrial, do you understand their decision-making processes and purchasing requirements?

5. If the customers are corporate, how large are they?

6. Are any of the customers in a troubled market?

7. Do they anticipate major changes in their industry that could affect their purchases from you?

8. Are the majority of the customers in a growing or expanding market?

9. What percentage of revenue do the top ten customers account for?

10. Is the business heavily dependent upon any one of these top ten?

11. Does the company have maintenance agreements or sales contracts? If so, when do they expire?

12. What kind of credit and payment history do these

customers have?

13. Are any of the customers government entities: state, federal, or local? If so, what are the payment terms?

The marketing program can make or break a company's business. If effective, it will bring profitability and success to the business; if ineffective, failure and business closure will often result. It is truly amazing when you consider the effect that a marketing program and campaign choices can have on a business; therefore, you as a new business owner should thoroughly examine the past marketing efforts and seek ways to improve on methods to reach prospective consumers.

1. Is demand for the product or service driven by basic necessity, or is it created through marketing?

2. Does the company have a formal marketing plan?

3. Has the company identified its target market? Has it been effective in reaching them?

4. Are the segments well defined and understood by current management?

5. Is there more than one definable market segment?

6. What kind of advertising is the company doing? Review any and all marketing contracts carefully.

7. What kind of literature, flyers, or brochures does the company distribute?

8. Have there been any news releases, press releases, or news articles about the company recently?

9. What channels are used to distribute products to market?

10. Is the product sold locally, regionally, or nationally?

11. Are changes occurring in the marketplace that could affect sales and/or distribution?

12. Are there other potential markets that the company could serve?

Your goal and mission in examining consumer and marketing information is not to determine just the negative aspects of the business, if there are any, but to identify areas of growth and expansion. Some of these areas will be quite obvious; others not so obvious until you've taken the time to review existing information and understand the industry you're entering.

Operations and facilities must be visited by you prior to any actual transactions of buy or sell. There have been many instances when a business looked like an extremely attractive buy on paper only to be a tremendous disappointment upon an actual visit. Businesses can and do make a business look better on paper than it actually is, so much so that a physical location visit can be an astonishing and disappointing revelation. The facility's structural condition, the condition of the equipment, and the operating environment shed light on the real value of a business. Never purchase a business until you first take the time to pay it a visit. If you're selling your business, make sure that you honestly disclose any information pertinent to the actual condition of your machinery, equipment, and operating facilities. And as with anything you are preparing for sale, put on the best face possible. Clean up your operations.

1. Does the company have modern equipment?

2. Is the equipment sufficiently serviced and maintained?

3. Is the equipment new, used, leased, or owned?

4. Is the facility owned, rented, or leased?

5. Are the facilities neat and clean?

6. What size is the facility?

7. Can the business be moved?

8. Does the company have a strategic plan?

9. Does the company have a quality control program?

10. At what capacity utilization rate is the company running?

11. How does the company measure productivity?

12. How does the company manage its operations?

Management should be a big concern for a buyer only if you don't intend to make major changes once you have completed the buy/sell transaction. Often, a new buyer will relieve management of their responsibilities immediately upon taking over. In small businesses, this is a very frequent occurrence.

1. Who is currently managing the day-to-day operations?

2. What is the organizational structure of the business?

3. To what extent is the current owner involved in operations? finance and marketing?

4. Does the owner play a crucial part in any aspect of the business?

5. Are there any specialized managers within the company?

6. What is the nature of the relationship between current management and the owner?

7. How well do your skills fit in with those of current management?

8. Do resources exist to complement your weaknesses, or do you have specific strengths that will augment current under-managed areas?

9. Do you plan to be an active owner or absentee owner?

10. How comfortable are you with the idea of managing this business?

11. Has the company had any employee-related lawsuits?

12. Do these people plan to stay after the acquisition?

13. What is the general record of current management?

14. Have they placed the company in a strategic position of leadership within the industry?

You cannot underestimate the importance of the previous owner's role and the role of key personnel in a small business. The very livelihood of the business is often a result of the personality and input, knowledge, and foresight of the small business owner. Therefore, the continued success of such a business may rely heavily upon the new owner's input; if you're not prepared for the role you will need to play, then you should give serious thought to the purchase prior to closing the deal. If possible, seek the continued support of the previous owner, either through contract and non-compete agreements, or through the use of earn-outs and/or buyout provisions in the buy/sell agreement.

Reasons for the sell can be as varied as the owners who have placed the business on the market. Some of these reasons can turn out to be totally irrelevant to your position as a prospective buyer; others can turn into the potential for a nightmarish journey straight to failure. Take the time to talk with the owner. Ask why the business is for sale; talk to employees, customers, vendors, and suppliers. You are placing a great deal of your life into a new commitment and more than likely a great deal of your personal wealth; make sure you're buying the business you believe yourself to be purchasing.

- Have you talked to competitors and industry experts to determine if there might be hidden reasons for the sale of the business?

- During the course of your due diligence and examination of the business records, did you turn up any suspicious information that might contradict the current owner's stated reasons for selling?

- Have you spoken with suppliers, customers, and employees to determine if they have any information detrimental to the sale of the business?

The information you're seeking here will not make you popular with current owners and management if you discover there are some oversights or half-truths, but you will be much better off in your quest for a business if you steer clear of troubled businesses, unless that's what you're looking to buy.

Legal and tax implications of the business are discussed only briefly here, as there is an entire chapter devoted to the definitions, relativity, and possible repercussions of liability involved in the buying and selling of a business. Your purpose at this point is to determine if there are any existing legal or tax problems, pending actions, bankruptcies, or litigation that could have a negative impact on the future of the business.

It is, however, very important that you understand the consequences of pending actions, tax liens, and any other contractually binding agreements that may exist prior to the sale of the business. Sometimes a change in ownership will relieve the business of prior contractual obligations, but more often than not, you will be expected to honor those existing obligations. If the business is sold intact as a legal entity, you can rest assured the sins of the previous owner or owners will be visited upon the new owner, namely you. This type of information does not necessarily eliminate the business as a prospective buy, but it does affect the value of the business and what you should be willing to pay in order to purchase it, along with the legal or other liabilities.

Legal questions to explore should include the following:

1. Does the company have any contracts or other legal obligations?

2. Do you plan to purchase the assets or the stock of the business? If so, purchase of the stock carries with it all the liabilities—past, present, or future—of the business.

3. Are there any current or pending lawsuits against the business that might prevent the transfer of operating assets?

4. If the business is a corporation, what vote is required on the part of the shareholders to sell assets of the business?

5. Do any of the assets have liens placed against them?

6. What is the seller's tax position?

7. What type of insurance does the company have?

8. How has the company depreciated assets, and will there by any tax liability upon a sale?

9. Who handles the taxes of the business?

10. Who is the company's attorney?

11. Do you know how the current owner's earnings are withdrawn from the company?

Now that you've taken the time to examine the non-financial issues surrounding the business, take a moment to visualize your plan for the business. How closely does your proposed method of operations match the current style of operations? Will your method of operation work with the current market, economic, growth, and management structure in place today?

Other issues that will play a role in determining the actual value of the business and what you may be acquiring when you purchase it are those that are more of an ethical or moral nature and must be evaluated on an individual basis.

Additional sources of information will be your state and local governments; if the business is incorporated, the corporate papers, bylaws, and officers will be public information. Dun and Bradstreet may also have a listing for the business and, if so, will reflect any liens that have been placed on the business either tax or court ordered because of judgments.

The greatest contributor to failure when you are buying and selling businesses is a lack of preparation and knowledge. It's not magic when an individual is successful. It's the result of preparing, looking ahead, and obtaining the knowledge to make a business successful. As you read these chapters and review the information provided here, it may at times seem overwhelming. Take it one chapter at a time. Read and re-read. Ask questions. Seek out businesspeople who have been or are currently successful business owners. Most are very willing to impart information, and you are going to need all of it. As we talk about markets, advertising, management, economics, and sales volume, please understand that whether you realize it or not, you will absorb this information and it will be an asset should you choose to buy or sell a business

Evaluating the Financial Health of a Business

When you reach this phase of the evaluation, you should consider using an accountant and possibly a tax attorney. This information can be quite overwhelming to work with, yet it is crucial that you develop an adequate picture of the exact financial health of the business. In this section, we're going to define some terms you need to be familiar with and give you examples of financial documents that you may need to look at. We'll also show you how to evaluate and use ratios when determining the health of the business, and what those ratios and evaluations will mean to you in negotiating a better price.

In the following paragraphs, we're going to begin by defining some of the most common terms.

Asset value of a business is the determined value of actual assets less the liabilities of the business. **Book value** is not the method used for valuation of the business assets; the book value of an asset is used to determine income tax assessments on the asset for purposes of depreciation and amortization. The **fair market value** should be used to determine the actual monetary value of an asset. There are other methods that can be used, and these were discussed briefly in Chapter 2. We won't address them in any further detail as the preferred and most common method of valuation is the fair-market-value price.

Distribution of assets refers to the actual distribution of the assets on the balance sheet. You have current and long-term assets, and there is a certain mix that is considered to be healthy. Normally, a 60-40 mix (60 percent current and 40 percent long-term) is the healthiest level attainable for small businesses. This, however, is not a steadfast rule. **Current assets** refer to cash, savings, and easily liquidated bonds or funds. **Long-term assets** are things like machinery and equipment and real estate.

Cash flow is generally the amount of money left over after the cost of goods, expenses, administrative, and other general selling costs are deducted, but prior to the deduction of taxes, interest, depreciation, and amortization. How does cash flow affect selling price?

Income capitalization is the method of converting future income into a present-day value. **Discounted cash flow methods** and **multiple cash flow methods** are used to determine the value of a business and operate on the belief that tomorrow's income will be worth less than the value of the income today. Examples of each method and the most recommended applications are presented below.

Retained earnings are the accumulated amounts of net income added each accounting period to the balance sheet and the value of the business. What do retained earnings say about a company, and what do small businesses traditionally do with any net income? The answer here is that very few small businesses will actually retain net income; generally, any remaining income is paid out at year end in the form of employee or management bonuses.

Historical financials are prior years' financial statements that give insight to many facets of the current operating conditions; both economic and market changes can be discerned through the examination of the financial history.

Cash versus **accrual method** of recordkeeping simply must be understood so that you can identify the method used and the status of any income relevant to your intended time of purchase and assumption. The method used will have very little bearing on the financial health of a small business.

Expenses are defined as the assets used up or services consumed in the process of generating revenue or income. Expenses are different from cost of goods sold in that they are not direct inputs in the manufacture or production process, but they are necessary for the operations. Expenses can be as costly to a business as the cost of goods sold, and are, therefore, included in this discussion.

The **financial statements** of the business can be compared to the central nervous system in a human being. They are the road map you need to determine where the business is coming from and potentially where it may be headed or possibly where you can take it. An explanation of each of the individual statements that come together to be known as the financial statements follow in the next few paragraphs.

The **statement of cash flows** is a summary of the major cash receipts and cash payments for a particular period of time. **Statement of owner's equity** is a summary of the changes in owner equity of a business that has occurred during a specific period of time. The **income statement**, also known as a **profit and loss sheet**, is a summary of the revenues and expenses of a business for a specific period of time (see Fig. 4.1). The **balance sheet** is a financial statement listing the assets, liabilities, and owner equity of a business for a specific period of time (see Fig. 4.2).

The following pages provide sample documents that will give you an idea as to what these financial documents look like. These will be used later in comparing percentages and ratios and what you should expect to see in a healthy business. The statement of cash flows and the owner's equity statements aren't included here simply because the information you're interested in obtaining will come from the income statement (profit and loss) and the balance sheet; therefore, we are only concerned with establishing familiarity with those financial documents.

Figure 4.1   **PROFIT AND LOSS**

	2005
Ordinary Income/Expense	
Income	
BONUS	500.00
	7,641.54
401 - Fees Earned	43,501.34
402 - Discounts	-1,497.50
Total Income	50,145.38
Expense	
Management Expense	10,400.00
501 - Rent Expense	134.00
502 - Utilities Expense	4,417.52
503 - Supplies Expense	1,810.79
504 - Insurance Expense	1,679.69
505 - Miscellaneous Expense	1,068.42
506 - Contract Services	8,321.48
507 - Advertising Expense	1,547.98
508 - Auto Expense	1,911.42
509 - Interest Expense	449.49
510 - Office Expense	4,123.33
512 - Repairs & Maintenance Expense	361.52
513 - Professional & Legal Fees	25.00
514 - Taxes & Licenses	1,173.17
515 - Operating Supplies Expense	897.47
519 - Merchant Services Expense	309.50
6999 - Uncategorized Expenses	366.00
Total Expense	38,996.78
Net Ordinary Income	11,148.60
Other Income/Expense	
Other Income	
403 - Rental Income	16,408.00
405 - Interest Income	129.77
Total Other Income	16,537.77
Net Other Income	16,537.77
Net Income	**27,686.37**

Figure 4.2   **BALANCE SHEET**

2005

ASSETS

  Current Assets

    Checking/Savings

101 - Checking Account	6,668.67
101-1 - Cash Account	3,000.00
101-2 - Savings Account	12,500.00
Total Checking/Savings	22,168.67
Accounts Receivable	
102 - *Accounts Receivable	389.00
Total Accounts Receivable	389.00
Other Current Assets	
110 - E-Trade Stocks	1,124.23
Total Other Current Assets	1,124.23
Total Current Assets	23,681.90
Fixed Assets	
181 - Buildings	36,000.00
182 - Office Equipment	12,305.00
Total Property & Equipment	48,305.00
184 - Investment Property	16,500.00
Total Fixed Assets	64,805.00
TOTAL ASSETS	**88,486.90**

LIABILITIES & EQUITY

  Liabilities

    Current Liabilities

      Accounts Payable

200 - *Accounts Payable	108.86
Total Accounts Payable	108.86
Credit Cards	
206 - VISA	6,488.03
Total Credit Cards	6,488.03
Total Current Liabilities	6,596.89
Total Liabilities	6,596.89
Equity	
300 - Opening Bal Equity	19,644.00
301 - Owner Capital	10,500.00
302 - Retained Earnings	24,059.64
Net Income	27,686.37
Total Equity	81,890.01
TOTAL LIABILITIES & EQUITY	**88,486.90**

FINANCIAL ANALYSIS

As you can see in the examples, a healthy business will have a positive net income and assets that outweigh liabilities. There will not always be the wide margin of difference that is shown here, but there should be evidence of more asset than liability. When you examine that information, if you determine that the business is making money but maybe not as much as is possible, how do you identify problem areas or areas that are ripe for improvement? You do this by using percentages and ratios. Most everyone you speak with (except an accountant or mathematician) will show some disdain at the mention of percentages and ratios. In reality, they are the keepers of the secrets when it comes to examining businesses. It would be in your best interest to pay close attention to how they work and why.

The business we're going to examine in the next few paragraphs is used for illustration only and is not intended for readers to use as the basis for evaluations; it will, however, give you a clear understanding of what you're looking for when you examine business financials and how to interpret the information you see. We're going to use a fictional company known as Best Box Buy, Inc. The background information on this business is as follows:

Best Box Buy, Inc. is a small family-owned business that has experienced an increase in sales over the last three years; however, the original founder died midyear during the first year of financial information we're examining, and the survivors have not been able to keep the business profitable. They've decided to sell the business. They have also made a great show of the fact that sales have continued to increase even with the death of the original founder. What are they not telling you?

The fastest way to put together a clear picture of business trends that have affected this business over the last few years is to do a vertical analysis of the balance sheet and the profit and loss statement over the last three years. This vertical analysis will look like the one shown in Figures 4.3 and 4.4.

Figure 4.3

ITEM	YEAR 1	YEAR 2	YEAR 3
Assets			
Cash	11%	7%	4%
Accounts Receivable	38%	42%	48%
Notes Receivable	5%	4%	0%
Inventory	13%	19%	25%
Prepaid Expenses	3%	3%	2%
Total Current Assets	70%	75%	80%
Land and Buildings	20%	17%	15%
Machinery and Equipment	10%	8%	7%
Less Depreciation	(2)	(2)	(2)
Goodwill	2%	2%	2%
Total Assets	100%	100%	100%
Liabilities			
Notes Payable	5%	3%	1%
Accounts Payable	20%	28%	35%
Taxes Payable	4%	3%	2%
Accruals	1%	2%	2%
Total Current Liabilities			
Capital			
Long-Term Debt	10%	12%	13%

ITEM	YEAR 1	YEAR 2	YEAR 3
Stock	40%	36%	32%
Paid-in-Surplus	20%	18%	15%
Total Capital	70%	66%	60%
Total Liabilities and Capital	100%	100%	100%

Figure 4.4

	YEAR 1	YEAR 2	YEAR 3
Gross Sales	100%	100%	100%
Less Returns/Allowances	(2%)	(3%)	(4%)
Net Sales	98%	97%	96%
Cost of Goods Sold			
Materials	(40%)	(41%)	(42%)
Labor	(20%)	(21%)	(22%)
Gross Profit	38%	35%	32%
General and Administrative Expense	(20%)	(20%)	(20%)
Selling Expenses	(10%)	(10%)	(10%)
Total Expenses	(30%)	(30%)	(30%)
Operating Profit	8%	5%	2%
Interest	(2%)	(3%)	(4%)
Taxes	(3%)	(2%)	(1%)
Net Profit After Tax	3%	0%	(3%)

What can we learn from this information?

Returns and allowances. Unless there is a real problem, returns and allowances should never be over 2 percent of gross sales. When you look at the numbers above, returns and allowances have risen each year; this could be indicative of a poor product and quality problems, a return policy that is too lenient, or a combination.

Analysis: Quality and return policy problems.

Gross profit. This is probably one of the most important items to address. If gross profit goes down, it should be because of dramatic increases in material costs. If the selling, general, and administrative costs (also known as fixed overhead expense) do not show a significant increase, you can operate profitably with a decrease in gross profit. However, over a three-year period, management should have found a way to offset higher materials and labor expense if in no other way, then by raising the selling price of the product.

Analysis: Management problems relating to lack of necessary cost analysis.

Selling, general, and administrative expenses (fixed overhead expense). If you're operating in a highly competitive market and cannot afford to increase selling prices, then you would generally seek to cut overhead or labor expense. Neither was done here.

Analysis: Management problems due to lack of overhead and labor analysis; additionally, this probably reflects salaries of family members unwilling to cut labor expense.

Accounts receivables. This area should be scrutinized not only for percentage value increases but also for the age of the accounts. As a general rule, if you see increases in the accounts receivables over the period of a year, there are either bad accounts or slow accounts.

Analysis: Operating cash is not being converted in a timely manner.

Inventory. This area along with your accounts receivables are two of the most important areas to manage well simply because they can tie up a vast amount of operating cash, and that can be very detrimental to business. In this scenario, inventory levels have almost doubled over the three years examined. An additional problem created by carrying a lot of inventory is the possibility of product obsolescence with lots of product still in stock.

Analysis: Production, scheduling, and management issues would seem apparent.

Long-term debt. Generally speaking, you only utilize long-term debt options to finance plant and equipment purchases. In this example, however, long-term debt has been incurred to finance a shortage of operating capital. There is an evident lack of long-term debt increase due to machinery and equipment purchases.

Analysis: Management has made an unsound business decision.

What can you summarize and assume just from these figures? I probably have the edge here, but I'll tell you what I see:

A small family business, run in large part by the founding owner; family members were included simply because of the fact that they were family. There may be one or two key family members but none who are able to manage the business with the same clout of the founder. Due to a lack of strong leadership and probably a great lack of experience, ingenuity, and intuition about the product or service provided, the company is operating with excessive waste, a lack of management direction, and no clear plan for turnaround. If you're looking for a business that is in need of a turnaround specialist, I'd say at first glance, this might be a great buy.

It's here that you are also given the chance to view what is known as pro forma statements. Pro forma statements provide the opportunity to get a glimpse of the possible effect of your anticipated changes on the business operations. The pro forma statements are operating statements that project the future performance of the business. They're the window to the business's future. They also are not for the novice entrepreneur to try to complete without the aid of an accountant or financial expert. The other objective you're concerned with in creating the pro forma statements is to determine the amount of free cash flow, or the amount of cash the business will generate during this projected future time. This is crucial information since one of the primary needs of the business will be adequate cash flow. You will see this term again when we discuss sensitivity and break-even analysis.

There are some additional items to look at after you've made the first run at the financials. There is something known as benchmarking that gives prospective buyers a chance to compare a single business with the industry average. This is accomplished using four major variables:

1. Volume

2. Inventory turnover

3. Overhead as a percentage of sells

4. Cost of capital

How do you bring this together to provide a meaningful number to compare against industry standards? You let your accountant do this for you. Since we only have ten chapters, and my teaching skills are limited, I am not going to turn this into an accounting and finance class. You need to be aware of this benchmarking process and request the information from your accountant during the due-diligence or other analysis process; just make sure you check the business against the industry average. If the business you're examining is well below the industry average along with the observations you make about the ratios shown before, caution is advised.

RATIOS

We're now going to look at some of the ratios you will need to use and why. Ratios are used to determine where the business falls in relation to other businesses or industry standards. They are a useful tool in assessing the financial health of the business and should be used by a prospective buyer to help determine the risk involved. They are also valuable once you have reached the negotiation table as a bargaining tool for a better price.

There are some basic ratios that you will want to check:

1. Balance sheet ratios

2. Operating ratios

3. Current ratios

4. Collection turnaround for accounts receivable

5. Inventory turnaround

6. Return on investment

These ratios are by no means comprehensive of the total number of ratios that can and are checked during the financial due diligence. These ratios, however, provide crucial information about the business; it is absolutely necessary that you understand them, know how and when to use them, and request the specific results during the financial due diligence.

The balance sheet ratios are the numbers and percentages we compared in Figures 4.3 and 4.4.

The operating ratios compare your expenses to your income levels. As a general rule, for each industry, just as with gross margins, there are industry averages for these comparisons.

Current ratios show the relationship between current assets and current liabilities. This is a way to check the ability of a business to meet its financial obligations (this is also known as solvency). An especially low number, or an examination of several years' financial statements that reveals a decline in that number, would be a good indicator of internal problems. One note of importance here: There is a form of current ratio that is known as the acid-test ratio. This will actually provide a better picture if you're trying to determine the actual ability of the company to pay its debts. The acid-test ratio is the measure of the quick assets, such as cash, to current liabilities. The higher the acid-test ratio, the better position a business is in to pay its current liabilities in a crisis situation.

Collection turnaround for accounts receivables indicates the average number of days it takes the business to collect on its accounts receivables. The longer it takes the company to collect, the longer operating capital is tied up and unavailable for use. Excessively high turnaround numbers indicate either a lack of adequate policy and personnel or slow-paying customers. Neither condition is conducive to profitable business.

Inventory turnaround refers to the amount of goods sold and

the dollar value of inventory. This ratio is computed by dividing the cost of goods sold by the average inventory. A higher number indicates that the company is in a good position for solvency and necessary operating capital is available. A lower number is indicative of too much inventory and a lack of good management in inventory levels.

Return on investment is one of the most important ratios; in fact, many business investors will tell you no other ratio is as important. I believe it all depends upon your individual goal. However, the ROI (return on investment) average for good, solid companies is between 18 and 20 percent. Venture capitalists and other "investment-only" individuals usually seek ROIs of 30 percent or greater.

That just about wraps up ratios. There are a couple of areas we need yet to cover. While they aren't ratios, they are cousins. For further explanation of ratios that are used in analyzing the overall health and financial condition of the business, see Figure 4.5. There are more ratios listed there; depending upon the type of business you are evaluating, you may or may not find them useful.

SENSITIVITY AND BREAK-EVEN ANALYSIS

Since all of the information you're gathering is based on the prior owner's historical financial data and the projected financials based on your business assumptions, you might want to perform the following analyses. These analyses are not necessary in your evaluation of business health or financial status. What they will do, however, is provide you with worst-case scenarios if your projections should turn out to be somewhat off the mark.

Sensitivity analysis refers to the sensitivity of the projections you made to the changes in underlying assumptions. When you made your projections on the pro forma format, you made them prior to being involved in the business; therefore, there is a high margin for error. When you perform a sensitivity analysis, you can alter your assumptions and see how these changes affect the bottom line. For example, if your pro forma projections included a sales increase of 10 percent per year for the next five years, what would happen if sales increased only 5 percent for the next three years? The sensitivity analysis allows you to look at all the possible variations in assumptions. In order to do a complete sensitivity analysis, you should modify the key variables one at a time. This helps you to see how vulnerable your net income will be to any changes that might occur. You should be able to use a computer and set up a program that will allow you to run the various scenarios.

Break-even analysis is another useful method for using the projected cash flows and the assumptions you've made to determine where you must be in order to break even. First, you must separate expenses into fixed and variable costs. Fixed costs remain constant regardless of the volume of business that is done. Variable costs are heavily reliant on the volume of goods produced. Packaging, assembly costs, shipping, and labor allocation are dependent upon the volume produced. Rent, equipment leases, insurance, and long-term debt are fixed costs. In order to determine the amount of revenue needed in order to break even, you should use the following formula and construct a graph that is used for break-even analysis:

Break-even = Fixed costs/(Revenue per unit - variable cost per unit)

If debt is used to finance the purchase, the fixed costs will rise, and this will in turn raise the break-even point. Changes in materials, labor, and other variable costs will create changes in the break-even level also. If nothing else, this type of analysis will make you more aware of the effect cost increases as well as long-term debt increases can have on your net income.

By now you should be thoroughly exhausted from examining and reviewing financial information, ratios, and analysis. If all of this seems a bit much, take the time to read the chapter once again. You will be surprised at how much you will learn just from a second reading. Also, take the information here and sit down with your accountant/financial advisor. There are terms used here that might not be explained to the depth that you want or need. Your financial advisor or accountant should be able to further explain as well as show you, based on information you're familiar with, just what these numbers, analyses, and ratios can mean to you.

Figure 4.5

RATIOS	
I. Liquidity	
Current Ratio =	Current assets / Current liabilities
Quick Ratio =	Current assets – Inventory / Current liabilities
Day's sales receivable =	Accounts receivable / Avg. credit sales per day
Day's payable =	Accounts payable / Avg. purchases per day
II. Capital Structure and Long-Term Solvency	

RATIOS	
Total debt to capital =	$$\frac{\text{Current liabilities} + \text{Long-term liability}}{\text{Equity capital} + \text{Total liabilities}}$$
Long-term debt to equity =	$$\frac{\text{Long-term liabilities}}{\text{Equity capital}}$$
III. Return on Investment and Profitability	
Return on assets =	$$\frac{\text{Net income} + \text{Interest expenses (1 - taxes)}}{\text{Average total assets}}$$
Return on equity =	$$\frac{\text{Net income}}{\text{Average equity}}$$
Gross margin =	$$\frac{\text{Gross profit}}{\text{Sales}}$$
Net income to sales =	$$\frac{\text{Net income}}{\text{Sales}}$$
Operating profits to sales =	$$\frac{\text{Operating profit}}{\text{Sales}}$$
IV. Turnover	
Inventory Turns =	$$\frac{\text{Sales or cost of goods sold}}{\text{Inventory}}$$

CASE STUDY

Denise's Flowers and Gifts, Inc. is a locally owned-and-operated flower and gift shop that fills a gap in a community starved for affordable gifts and a continually operating flower service.

Contact Information: **Denise Williams**
12053 Hwy. 96
Millport, AL 35576

I started Denise's Flower and Gifts, Inc. because I recognized a need in the community and I had the resources to start a new business. In addition to my customer service experience, I also had family who knew flowers and could operate the shop. Financially, I enjoy the extra income, and I feel as though I'm providing my community with a needed resource.

However, it has taken some real sacrifice on my and my husband's part to pull together a new business and get it off the ground while holding down our regular jobs. Finding the initial investment was also somewhat of a challenge, so we borrowed the startup money. Our accountant and the local banker helped us with financing and tax issues.

Although I've never sold a business, I believe customer loyalty and an excellent business reputation adds tremendously to the total value of the business. Starting and running a business has been a great learning experience, and we would certainly do it again.

CHAPTER 5

THE VALUE OF A BUSINESS

Key issues covered in this chapter include:

- *Valuation Techniques*
- *Business Appraisers and the Valuation Process*
- *Valuation Worksheets*

Once you have obtained the financial documentation you need and have access to the listed assets, the accounts to be considered, book values, and almost any other piece of financial data, you can begin to put together a picture of the actual price you can ask or offer during the buy/sell process. I can't stress too much the importance of the due-diligence process and the information you will need to review, examine, and then review once more. Chapters 4 and 5 cover some of the most important information you will need during this process. Make sure you have either a thorough understanding of accounting and financials or that you have a competent professional on your acquisition team.

This is the single-most important area for determining a value, and many potential buyers and sellers fail to spend enough time here or do a thorough job when investigating the business. You must have extensive knowledge of the value of real estate prices in the surrounding area, new/used equipment pricing, the condition of the proposed business, and an estimated average of repair/reconditioning expense that is associated with a particular business during a buy or sell. If the business is in a service industry, how much of the potential value is leaving with the former owner? How much of the valuation is based on previous sales dollars and potential sales dollars? All of the factors must be considered when pricing a business regardless whether your position is buyer or seller.

VALUATION TECHNIQUES

The following section examines the most popular methods used to value a business, and provides diagrams and illustrations necessary for performing the analysis. There are also suggested methods for determining the value of intangibles such as goodwill. The most beneficial choice, but decidedly the most often overlooked, is the decision to hire a professional business appraiser. Professional business appraisers make their livings valuing small businesses. They are often the most qualified individuals to make an accurate appraisal, a financially beneficial asset for prospective buyers or sellers. Many states have regulations in place that establish certain criteria that professional appraisers must meet prior to being allowed to call themselves professional business appraisers. Screen any possible candidates prior to hiring them and check their credentials. The legitimate business appraiser will normally be a member of the Institute of Business Appraisers or the American Society of Appraisers; at least you can be assured if the individual is a member that he or she is aware of the standards that govern business appraisal.

The additional benefit derived from hiring professionals is that they are aware of the different methods that may be used to determine the value of a business and will be able to guide you in your decision as to which method you should use. Once a value has been determined, can you be assured that this will be the eventual price given or accepted for the sale of the business? Absolutely not; the valuation of a business is simply a baseline for you and the buyer or seller, as the case may be, to begin negotiations and for you to determine whether a negotiated price is appropriate or simply does not make good financial sense, at which point you should walk away.

In determining which valuation method should be used, you need to understand all the different options that are available and then make a choice. Basically, there are only two tangible components in determining the value of an operating business: the assets that are used to produce income, and the cash flow that results from the use of those assets. Therefore, you have the asset- or cost-based valuation and you have the cash flow or income valuation. Although there are some middle-road methods such as price to earnings and price to cash flow, we will not, for the purposes of buying and selling small businesses, be concerned with these methods; they are generally used for large, publicly traded companies. We will begin with the asset-based approach.

The asset- or cost-based approach will use one of several formulas: the fair-market-value, the liquidation value, or the book-value method, and some of these methods will incorporate the use of goodwill simply as a way to beef up the value of the business. Let's take a look at each of these methods, and then we'll examine the use of goodwill in the last paragraphs so that we understand how and why it is sometimes incorporated.

The fair-market-value approach is the most-often-used method for determining the asset value of the business, and will most typically include some reasonable value of goodwill. Since this is the most-often-used method, it also requires that the value be set by a professional business appraiser or, at the very least, a knowledgeable person in the particular business area. In order to establish a fair market value, each asset included in the sale must be examined, financially and physically. In order to establish the fair market value, you need access to the balance sheet and the business establishment. Quite often, with small family businesses, there are assets on the grounds that are not included as separate balance-sheet items. There is also the possibility that what you see is not what you get. At this juncture, you should ask pointed questions about the assets that are included in the sale and determine exactly what you will receive so that you can establish a legitimate fair market value.

The first account listed under assets, of course, would be cash. Believe it or not, you should always ask how the cash asset of the business will be handled. Does the current owner intend to keep the cash account, or will it be a part of the business sale? More often than not, the cash accounts will be retained by the seller. If the cash is not retained, make sure there are no restrictions placed on the use of the cash; sometimes, financial institutions require minimum balances, or the cash may be tied to a liability as a form of collateral. You can see how the exclusion of the cash asset, should the cash be valued at say, $15,000, would affect the actual value of the business you are buying.

The next item for consideration, and it is here that a thorough amount of due diligence should be performed, concerns the accounts receivable. Every business, no matter how large or small, has accounts receivable that are stale or may never be collected. Publicly traded companies are required to remove old accounts at the end of a certain period of time; small businesses that are privately held, however, are not required to follow the same regulations. During the performance of the due diligence, ask some pointed questions about the accounts receivables. If you are purchasing the accounts receivables, you need to be aware of the value of accounts that may never be collected; if a large majority of these accounts are personal accounts, I would suggest that you simply choose not to purchase the accounts receivable.

In some cases, the accounts receivables may be used during the negotiations for reducing the selling price, if included in the sale. At any rate, make sure you understand the age and exact value of the accounts receivable, and if there are any special considerations between the current owners and the customers. You can also enlist the services of a receivables lender or factor. These individuals or companies buy accounts receivables. That is their line of business and it is sometimes well worth the expense to pay for a company to evaluate the fair market value of the receivables, especially if receivables are a considerable part of the assets. Use this as your base value for the accounts receivables and a bargaining tool.

Many of the same considerations that apply to accounts receivables also apply to valuation of the inventory. Depending upon the nature of the business you are valuing, the various stages of inventory have different levels of value. Raw materials, for instance, are fairly easy to value. Nothing has changed in their condition since being purchased from a vendor. It is quite easy to establish a current market value. Work in process, however, is much harder to pinpoint, simply because it's not a product that has been sold or purchased in its current condition; the company has affixed a labor value to the product, but it cannot be readily converted to cash at the value placed on the work in process per the company's books. The best way to determine the value here is to check with other companies that manufacture the same or a similar product to determine if the product can be sold in various stages, and what the actual market value would be. Finished goods are much easier to value and are more valuable to a business as a sellable item. The finished goods are ready for market and can quickly be sold, thereby converting inventory to a liquid asset of cash. In performing your due diligence, you should make it a point to actually visit the business location. Again, there are items that may or may not be listed on the inventory book value that have little or no actual market value. Identify and account for all goods that have been used to value inventory. Be absolutely certain that you can sell what you're purchasing at the value specified. Obsolete inventory, damaged inventory, or inventory items that are industry-specific cannot be included in the inventory value for sale purposes; or if they are included, it must be at an extremely reduced value.

One of the less obvious assets that are acquired during the purchase or sale of a business is prepaid rents and insurance. These are assets that can be valued based on the monetary preset investment. The only variable you should thoroughly check here is the continued validity of the prepaid investment. Can the insurance and lease be transferred upon the sale of the business? Will the current lease or rent levels remain the same long enough after the sale for there to be an actual benefit derived? If the answers to these questions are not readily available, make sure you spend the proper amount of time in obtaining the answers. Leases or insurance payments that will not remain at current levels—that may double in just a few months, for example—are no real benefit to the purchaser. It is also here where a professional appraiser would have the necessary forethought and vision to ask and receive lease, rental, and insurance information to be included or excluded in the business valuation process.

Those items sufficiently cover any current assets listed on the balance sheet. Although there may be others depending upon the business you are evaluating, these are the basic and generic items found on almost any balance sheet. Let's move now into the fixed asset valuation.

Fixed assets are things such as equipment, fixtures, buildings, furniture, etc., that are a fixed part of the business. They are not easily liquidated and they're not for sale, but they are necessary to the operation. The first to be examined is the equipment. At this juncture, you should request a detailed listing of any equipment that is included in the category and that has been included in the book value for the balance sheet. There should be a listing of all major pieces of equipment along with the actual or estimated book value. The condition of the equipment, the life expectancy of the equipment, and any notable deterioration of any of the equipment should be brought to the attention either of yourself or your business appraiser. This is an area where the professional business appraiser can make the greatest contribution. He or she should have an excellent working knowledge of the actual fair market value of the equipment, how to obtain the same or better equipment from another business or professional appraiser or auctioneer, and what that means to the valuation of the business. Highly specialized pieces of equipment would be harder to assess with a value, but they are also harder to obtain, which increases their value. Since many businesses have higher book values than fair market values assigned to the equipment, there will often be discrepancies here when trying to come to an agreeable purchase or sale price.

One other area that will often be included in the fixed asset value is the value of any furniture and fixed assets that are not equipment but are involved in the direct operation of the business. Examine this area closely. Will any benefit be derived from this asset by the new owner? If the answer is no, either disallow the value or use a very reserved estimate. If the assets can be purchased easily on a secondary, used, or liquidation basis, establish the value based on information obtained from an outside source.

Any fixed assets that the former owner will expect to retain upon selling the business should be established at this juncture and the value associated with those assets deducted from the business valuation. It is not required but beneficial to both parties involved if there is an official and agreed-upon listing of the exact pieces of equipment and other assets that will be transferred upon the closing of the deal.

Quite often, once the business valuation is complete and the appraiser's valuation is compared to the balance sheet (the business's book value of the business is shown here), the figures do not match (see Fig. 5.1). The book value of a business is often higher than the appraised valuation at fair market value because depreciation rates for businesses and the actual street value of the equipment often vary widely; and when you are preparing to buy or sell a business, the book value is not a realistic assessment of the dollar value of the assets.

You need to be aware at this point, if the buy/sell agreement is for the stock purchase of a company, liabilities must be included in the appraisal valuation. If the buy/sell agreement is simply for the purchase of the assets of the business, liabilities are not a factor. A clear, concise understanding of the agreed-upon form of purchase must be determined at this time.

An alternative method, one that is used about as often, is the method known as liquidation value. It is similar to the fair-market-value method with one exception: the liquidation method assumes an immediate need to sell. If you've done your homework, you will know which method you can use to value the business. When a business is in trouble and assets must be dissolved in order to clear the debts of the business, the seller is at a tremendous disadvantage. Of course, any thought for profit is purely luck; the need at this point is to shed assets and debt simply to clear the slate. Realizing a profit is not the objective.

When using the liquidation-value method for establishing the value of the business, you are assuming the value most likely to be obtained in the open market just as with fair market value except that you must sell immediately. This also devalues the assets immediately. Quite often, the liquidation value on assets falls between 50 and 75 percent, depending upon the assets. Cash, of course, retains its face value, no matter the situation. Accounts receivables will generally only bring about 50 percent of their net worth and inventory somewhere around 75 percent. Prepaid leases and insurance, assuming there is some refundable part of each, would be worth only the dollar value of the refund; normally, this is 20 percent, assuming the lease can be turned into a sublease. The fixed assets, such as furniture, equipment, and building, would yield about 50 percent of their book value, so purchasing a business in a liquidation situation yields extremely good purchasing power, but you must consider the negative aspect: If the business weren't in trouble, there would be no need for liquidation. You probably aren't buying a business that can be operated profitably any time soon, if ever, so you must assume that you might possibly be forced to follow this same pattern. For purposes of illustration, we will provide you with a table of comparison between the listed or book value of a business, the fair market value of the business, and the liquidation value of a business.

Figure 5.1

ASSET	LISTED/BOOK VALUE	FAIR MARKET VALUE	LIQUIDATION VALUE
Cash	$15,000.00	$15,000.00	$15,000.00
Accounts Receivable	$25,000.00	$20,000.00	$12,500.00
Inventory	$65,000.00	$63,000.00	$52,000.00
Prepaid Rents/Ins.	$5,000.00	$5,000.00	$1,000.00
Fixed Assets			
Equipment	$54,000.00	$44,300.00	$27,000.00
Fixtures/Bldgs.	$48,000.00	$41,200.00	$22,000.00
Other	$8,000.00	$5,500.00	$1,000.00
Total	$220,000.00	$194,000.00	$130,500.00

As you can see, the value of the business depends in large part on the timing of the purchase and the condition and distribution of the valuables.

Book value method for valuation is not used for determining the selling price of a business so much as it is used to support either a fair market value or a liquidation value. The book valuation of equipment and other fixed assets is used more for tax-reporting purposes and depreciation of the business than for actual business valuation in a buy/sell arrangement. It can, however, be used to compare and aid in establishing the fair market and liquidation values.

Upon reaching a valuation for the tangible assets, and depending upon the business's individual situation, you may or may not find it necessary to include a value for the intangibles such as goodwill, income, or cash flow. This valuation is also known as the time-value-of-money concept (multiple method and discounted method) and the use of customer lists to establish value. Each of these intangibles will be discussed in depth below due to the important role the intangibles play in the process of valuation.

Goodwill receives recognition here because many business owners will place a value on their businesses that exceeds the actual asset value. Goodwill is the difference between the asking price and the actual asset-value price. An understanding of the manner in which goodwill can affect your negotiations as well as your tax liability in the future is necessary in order for you to accurately assess the financial impact for the owner and the prospective buyer.

Often, as you enter a situation for buying or selling a business, the price being asked exceeds the valuation placed on the business using the asset approach. How does the seller arrive at that price? He or she has incorporated the goodwill factor into the asking price of the business. What does goodwill include? The reputation of the business, the name recognition of the business, and customer loyalty (often defended with customer lists). These are intangible assets but are, nonetheless, important in determining the value of the business. You will see the goodwill value used most often with service businesses, as most of the value is usually derived from the intangibles of employee expertise and customer loyalty. If you use the asset-based approach to value the business, goodwill cannot be depreciated for tax purposes, and many lenders will not lend money based on the goodwill of the business. While the cost-based approach does not allow for the inclusion of the goodwill value as a depreciable asset, the income-based approach to valuation does. It will be discussed in the next few paragraphs.

The cash flow or income-valuation method is the most-often-used method for valuing a small business today. Although it is sometimes necessary to know the asset value of the business, it is often more important to understand the ability of the assets to generate income. When you use the cash flow or income-valuation method, you are placing a value on the past or future cash flows of the business.

In order to fully understand how and why this method is used, you must understand the time-value-of-money principle. The time value of money is a generally accepted premise that a dollar today is worth more than a dollar tomorrow, and a dollar yesterday was worth more than a dollar today, based on the common-sense theory that if you have a dollar today, you can choose to use that dollar to make money whereas without that dollar, you have no means of generating income. This is the principle upon which the business of lending was established. To borrow and be able to do something with a dollar today and repay it with interest at some point in the future, enables the borrower to make money today. This principle is used today to negotiate buyouts that include future cash payouts to the former owner based on the future cash flows and dollar value of the business. This brings us now to the income-based methods of valuation that use the past and future cash flows of a business in determining a present value.

Cash flow or income-based valuation is divided into two basic methods for determining a value: the multiple method or the discounted cash flow method. The multiple method is the one most commonly used for determining the value of a profitable business; the key word here is profitable. If the business isn't profitable (on paper), then the multiple method cannot be used. It is then that the valuation must rely on the asset-based approach. We will first examine the multiple method, and then move to the discounted cash flow method in order to give the reader some education in both.

The multiple method, also known as EBIT (earnings before interest and taxes) is fairly simple and is quite straightforward in the formula that is used to determine a value. You begin with the most recent year's cash flow number (you will need access to the business's financial statements at this point), and that figure is then multiplied by an arbitrary number that is applied to the particular industry you are examining. Hence the name multiple method. There are some other factors that must be taken into consideration when you are arriving at your cash flow number; items such as excess owner's compensation, depreciation, amortization, increases or decreases in working capital, investment expenditures, and interest expenses must be added back to the net cash flow number. The multiple you use can be determined a number of ways; the unfortunate truth is that it is often the result of a comparison of the sale of similar businesses, and the multiple used for those particular sales will be the multiple applied in your instance. This is not the most accurate way; it is, however, fairly accurate in its business application and so continues to be used in this manner.

Sometimes the best way to determine the multiple that would be applied to your business is simply to ask others in your same line of work; quite often, even if they haven't themselves bought or sold a business, they know of someone who has and may be able to pass along some useful information. If this is not an option, check with professional business appraisers in your area. They will be sure to know of comparables in your area.

The problem with this method, and really the only problem you will encounter here, is that businesses used as comparables may have very little in common other than that they sell the same or closely related goods and services. Were both businesses profitable and growing? What if the income of the business has been declining, not growing? What if the assets of one business are much older than those of another, yet the income produced is greater? Sometimes the peculiarities of a business can actually justify the use of a different method, but the multiple for this particular method does not change.

This is a limitation of the multiple method in that it examines the historical financial data of a business; it does not consider the asset value, the age of the assets, or any particular changes in the business environment or economics. If you examine the information in the EBIT/Multiples Method Chart in Figure 5.2, you can reasonably deduct that during the year of 2003, some capital investment or other major improvement in the process occurred. What you cannot do is to determine the specifics of the improvements.

As you can see, buying or selling a business requires a vast amount of knowledge about the business you are proposing to buy or sell. Simple formulas or simple solutions will not be the best way to determine the value of a business or the buy/sell value of a business. The best advice when performing due diligence and trying to determine an accurate value for a business is to use several different methods and come up with a price range, a low-end to high-end expected value.

For a more detailed look at the EBIT/multiple method, examine the chart below:

Figure 5.2

	2001	2002	2003	2004
Revenue	$175,000	$184,000	$198,000	$225,000
Cost of Goods Sold	71,418	91,325	101,881	106,409
Gross Margin	$103,582	$ 92,675	$ 96,119	$118,591
Expenses:				
Supplies	402	318	617	688
Advertising	600	400	800	800
Rent	11,100	11,100	11,100	11,100
Labor/Wages	8,418	10,206	14,889	17,903
Salaries	52,000	52,000	52,000	52,000
Insurance	4,562	6,118	6,903	7,614
Utilities				
Electric	3,680	3,220	3,403	3,314
Phone	1,294	1,343	1,382	1,218
Depreciation	6,001	5,349	8,810	7,413
Total Expense	88,057	90,054	99,904	102,050
Earnings Before Int. & Taxes	**15,525**	**2,621**	**(3,785)**	**16,541**
Interest	3,600	3,018	5,409	4,876
Taxes	3,033	3,148	3,361	3,714
Net Income	**8,892**	**(3,545)**	**(12,555)**	**7,951**
Add-Backs for Free Cash Flow:				
Interest	3,600	3,018	5,409	4,876

	2001	2002	2003	2004
Depreciation	6,001	5,349	8,810	7,413
Excess Owner's Comp.	26,000	26,000	26,000	26,000
Free Cash Flow	$44,493	$30,822	$27,664	$46,240
Net Present Value Using Multiple Method of 5	$222,465	$154,110	$138,320	$231,200

There are some general rules of thumb when it comes to "across the board" EBIT multiples:

1. The most common multiple for industrial companies is 5 to 7; for retail sales 8; and 7 to 9 for initial public offering companies.

2. Often, buyers will pay up to 7 times EBIT for stand-alone companies, but only 4 to 5 times for add-on acquisitions.

3. The less you pay to purchase a business, the more you can offer as management incentives and the more you are able to pull from the business each year as a return on your investment.

The discounted cash flow method is another less-used but just-as-reliable method for determining shareholder value and larger companies' buy/sell valuation. Here's how the discounted cash flow method works: the discounted-cash-flow value of a business is the price someone is willing to pay today for the anticipated cash flow in future years. This is a method used most often in the financial world—by banks, accounting firms, and various other lending institutions. It is slightly more complicated than the multiples method but does account for the opportunity cost of capital. This opportunity cost of capital is the return you could earn by investing your money elsewhere. We mention this method here only for the sake of providing the reader with the knowledge that this method exists; for small businesses, the multiples method or the asset-based-valuation methods are the two most often used and most reliable methods for reaching a realistic buy/sell valuation.

The only loophole business that usually will not work with either the multiples, the discounted cash flow, or the asset-based valuation is the service company. These companies' most valuable assets are often the employees and the customers. Both are intangible assets, usually valued in a goodwill valuation that simply is intended to add value to the existing tangible assets. If you are prospecting with service-based companies, the most successful approach you can use is the multiple method with payouts structured over a three- to five-year period contingent upon the retention of major accounts. The multiples method, although not entirely foolproof, is perhaps the most accurate method for placing a value on a service business, but let me caution you again that any person who is considering the purchase or sale of a business should investigate more than one method for determining a range of value; it is through the performance of due diligence, different methods of valuation, and extensive knowledge about the industry you are interested in acquiring or selling that you will be able to establish a realistic value for a particular business.

BUSINESS APPRAISERS AND THE VALUATION PROCESS

Now that we've discussed all the different methods and

techniques used to perform the business valuation, let's take a look at the application of those methods and the process by which the individual appraiser performs that valuation. In almost nine out of ten cases, when a small business fails, the reason can be traced back to the fact that the buyer paid too much for the business, thus crippling his or her ability to succeed. If you're willing to pay several hundred thousand dollars for a business, or even several million dollars, you would think that paying a professional business appraiser a couple of hundred dollars per hour to perform an accurate evaluation would be seen as an excellent investment, but this is not always so.

Many buyers aren't willing to invest such a small amount as the average $200 per hour that an appraiser might charge to evaluate a million-dollar investment that just might fail. It is that point where many buyers and sellers make a mistake in their purchase or asking price. If you are the seller, this might not be a huge mistake, especially if the deal closes. However, if you're the purchaser, this can be a very costly mistake, one that eventually costs you the business. There are three key resources that you could use to help you that range from fairly expensive to very reasonable: The professional business appraiser, the common-sense business valuation, and astuteness as a buyer are all ways to prevent a failed negotiation or a failed business venture.

Professional business appraisers make their livings assessing the value of businesses. They are often the best-qualified individuals to make accurate and therefore financially beneficial assessments for prospective buyers or sellers. Professional appraisers in many states are required by regulation to meet certain criteria before they can call themselves professional business appraisers. Screen candidates prior to hiring them and check their credentials. The legitimate business appraiser will normally be a member of the Institute of Business Appraisers or the American Society of Appraisers. If the individual is a member, you can be assured that he or she is aware of the standards that govern business appraisal.

The additional benefit derived from hiring professionals is that they are aware of the different methods that may be used to determine the value of a business and will be able to guide you in your decision as to which method you should use. The professional, however, is not the only individual who is familiar with the standard valuation techniques and is not the only one who can give you a qualified valuation.

The common-sense business evaluator is sometimes as well qualified even if he or she is not licensed. This should be someone very familiar with the buying and selling of businesses and who has the networking contacts necessary to obtain excellent and up-to-date information about businesses in the area. The common-sense valuation can be valid so long as the evaluator documents the necessary conversations, data input, and statistics used to support the final valuation. Sometimes just as beneficial in determining the business valuation is astuteness on the part of the buyer. If you're the buyer, you must realize the significance of the moment. You are about to invest thousands, if not millions, of dollars in a business. It is in your best interest to know everything there is to know about that business. You have every right to ascertain that your investment is a wise one. Don't hesitate to question current owners, employees, and vendors. A business that is in good health and has all the necessary selling components in place will encourage buyer education, especially if that buyer has signed a confidentiality agreement. The seller has nothing to fear and everything to gain by providing the necessary information.

There are a few questions you should ask yourself no matter what the business valuation results:

1. Is the acquisition process worth the effort involved for this business?

2. Is the information reported concerning earnings really there? How can I be sure?

3. Am I going to be able to continue the rate of earnings once the business is purchased?

Any evidence found to the contrary should throw up red flags, and if I were the investor, I would re-think my offer even if the business valuation looks positive. There may be underlying elements that would render the financial findings such as the dollar value of the business irrelevant.

When you use an individual to assess the business and determine a valuation, there are some key factors he or she will use in coming to this conclusion. As an astute buyer, you should at least be familiar with the process and keep track of what your appraiser is doing. The following paragraphs will familiarize you with the process. Now that you have an understanding of the elements and the formulas used, you can better understand the complete process. When valuing a company, an appraiser will usually complete a three- to five-step process:

1. He or she will complete a thorough due-diligence examination of the quality of the earnings reported using the EBIT multiple method. The appraiser will look for add-backs that are not factored into the true earning power of the business. Every business encounters one-time expenses, but this should not be a

lengthy list. The add-backs should be standard items, normally only three, and should not skew the real earning potential.

2. In valuing the goodwill items, customer lists, name recognition, and other intangible assets, is the business going to be able to sustain this earnings rate? In other words, are there any hidden economic factors or environmental factors that are contributing to the desire to sell or buy this business that will affect earnings potential?

3. In performing the due diligence associated with valuing the business financials, earnings, assets, physical condition of assets, and any other direct correlation of information furnished to actual operations, the effective business appraiser will verify the information, using all means possible.

4. Are there any outstanding agreements between the current owner and customers or employees that would affect the earning potential or potential cash flow of the business? Is there any property that will leave with the current owner? This can be a very crucial non-financial and non-asset factor when you actually reach a valuation of the business. Employees who make necessary and profitable contributions to the business but are not going to stay can make a tremendous difference in the profitability of the business.

5. The business valuation is not complete until there has been a comparison of several different valuation methods, and an inclusion of any non-financial

information factored into the equation. As the last step involved, a thorough and effective business evaluator will perform a complete analysis of all the information gathered and apprise the buyer or seller of the best valuation estimate based on all the information available.

I am including a valuation worksheet here as a means of educating the prospective buyer or seller in becoming familiar with the complete process of business valuation and what to expect when you engage the services of a business appraiser. This worksheet is meant to act as a checklist for the appraiser so that all areas are covered and every element checked. Then due diligence can be an assured and complete process.

VALUATION WORKSHEET

1. Begin with the business. Identify the elements in the environment and the economy that give the business value; what elements detract from the business value? This is a pro-and-con look at the characteristics of the business in the current operating environment that work for the business and the elements that work against the business.

2. Items to be considered here would be the business market, the growth potential, technological advantages/disadvantages, customer base, asset value in relation to current market trends, management, historical data (including financials), the current size of the business, and the environmental and economic positives and negatives in relation to the area.

3. Perform a financial analysis of the business using several different methods in order to set a market range for low-end and high-end valuation. This process is not to be confused with the due diligence that is performed during the buy/sell process. This financial analysis is used to set a market valuation of the business; in using the EBIT method for valuation, a financial analysis must be performed in order to arrive at the free-cash-flow value.

4. Examine the business from a market standpoint. Consider the indicators that point to high value and consider the indicators that point to a lower value such as the facility's condition; the local economy in relation to employee base; federal and local taxes and regulations; environmental regulations; changes in the industry; competitors; stability of the industry; debt of the individual business in comparison with other businesses in the same industry; asset condition in comparison to competitors in the same industry; and any upcoming major process, material, or equipment changes.

5. Get a second opinion. Quite often, the business appraisers themselves will seek a second opinion, especially if there is some questionable aspect of the valuation.

6. Provide the prospective buyer or seller with the information developed and the best structure and terms for buyout in the appraiser's opinion based solely on the facts obtained during the valuation process. Often, an appraiser will determine that

equipment changes, economic changes, or some other change that could produce a noticeable impact on the business are likely to occur, and that is invaluable information when negotiating a deal and structuring a buyout agreement.

Now that we've come to the end of this somewhat lengthy chapter on business valuations, let's take a few closing paragraphs to recap the information contained here and summarize the chapter as a whole. Upon finishing this chapter, I would suggest that you re-read this information. There is so much to be learned here and so much information that the average investor may or may not be familiar with, especially when applying this information to a particular business, that it merits a review.

There are several methods that can be used to value a business; the most common are the asset- or cost-based approach of the fair-market-value method and the cash flow- or income-based approach of the multiples method. These are the most-often-used methods and should be used in conjunction to derive a low-end to high-end valuation of a business. The one thing to remember in using these methods is that the multiples method will only work if the business is in a profitable state.

There are established industry values that are used in conjunction with the multiples method, and very rarely does a prospective buyer or seller want to stray from these preset values.

The only business that does not seem to work well with either of these methods is the service industry. Service businesses are usually highly specialized and require the expertise of the owner, founder, or other personnel in order to succeed. The customer-loyalty factor in these types of businesses plays a huge role in whether or not they will succeed. Quite often, buyouts in this type of situation are structured to occur over a three- to five-year period and require the present owner to remain with the business for "x" number of years.

Hiring a professional business appraiser is the best way to assure that the value that is asked and that is paid is the most accurate and profitable for the buyer or seller. Professional appraisers are very inexpensive when compared to the possibility of a failed business venture that loses thousands of dollars for the investor. There are certain guidelines that these appraisers use in valuing a business; and as a prospective buyer or seller, you should be familiar with the elements used in valuing the business as well as the process. The best asset a buyer or seller can have is to be astute, informed, and committed.

If you will take the time to compare the information found in the asset-based valuation to the information obtained from the income-based valuation, you can see that the asset-based valuation is slightly lower than the income-based valuation. This is normal and is the reason the two should be used to establish a low- and high-end range of value that gives the prospective buyer or seller a starting point for the negotiations.

CASE STUDY

Greg's Pallets came into existence as a means to utilize leftover lumber from the family sawmill business.

Contact Information: Greg Webster
P.O. Box 1199
Vernon, AL 35592

I became a business owner because I wanted to be self-employed. My family has been in the sawmill business for years. Having grown up in and around it, I knew it was an ideal business to start. Owning a small business has allowed my family to prosper and to grow, as well as to create new business and new jobs in the community.

However, there have been some disadvantages. To date, the business has yet to generate a profit; we're still paying for the extra equipment. It took a lot of money to get the business started, and the politics involved were challenging. I feel, though, that the business has benefited the local economy.

Because this business is a spin-off of an existing family business, we didn't have to go through due diligence. I did seek financing, and my accountant and local banker handled each legal aspect of getting the business off of the ground.

I brought my knowledge of the sawmill business and a good work ethic to my business. For those considering starting a business, do your homework. Look at the numbers, and carefully review the economics of the surrounding community.

CLASSIFIED CASE STUDIES
TM
directly from the experts

CHAPTER 6

THE PROFIT

Key issues covered in discussing the methods used to attain the most profit possible are:

- *Maximizing the Profit*
- *As a Buyer*
- *As a Seller*
- *Key Issues of Profitability for Buyers or Sellers*

I f you're a buyer, the profit levels are as much a concern for you as for the seller; any profit to be had will quite naturally increase the buying or selling price, depending upon your position. If you're the seller, this is money in your pocket; if you're the buyer, it means it will require a greater investment, usually equating to additional capital. So how do you reach the maximum profit figure? Whether you are buyer or seller, you need to be as knowledgeable as your opponent and prepared to stand your ground.

MAXIMIZING THE PROFIT

Making the most of the opportunity you're given will generally include a lot of hard work; a buying or selling opportunity is no different. In order to fully capitalize on this kind of opportunity, you're going to need nerves of steel and a lot of information. The steps you will take to prepare for your position as a buyer or seller are not that vastly different. But this area of profit is a crossroads, and you each go in opposite directions. This chapter will take a look at the process of maximizing profit from a buyer's standpoint and that of a seller.

As a Buyer

Know your valuation information, the history of the company, the current financial status of the owner, and the major economic factors that affect the proposed business. If the seller has a weak spot, make sure you know what it is and that you're in a position to capitalize on that fact. Use your intermediary and your acquisition team to their fullest ability. Expert and professional opinions can go a long way in an effort to sway a seller.

As a Seller

A tremendous amount of forethought, planning, and attention to detail will net you a greater profit, especially if you can stand firm on the value of your business and your business practices. Take the time to familiarize yourself with the details involved in preparing your business for an excellent selling position. Present spotless financials, set firm limits for negotiations, establish a time frame for expected completion from beginning to close, and use your intermediary and professional advisors to their greatest capacity. Know your buyer and research his or her reasons for buying. A clear understanding of the buyer's motive will tell you exactly where you stand when negotiating a selling price, especially one that will include a sizable profit.

KEY ISSUES OF PROFITABILITY FOR BUYERS OR SELLERS

Other than the wisdom imparted in the previous paragraphs, the information you need as a buyer or seller in determining profitability levels is one and the same. The only difference is the viewpoint. The buyer hopes to achieve the lowest price possible, thereby reducing profit, and the seller operates at the other end of the spectrum. The knowledge you need to maximize or minimize on the profit level doesn't change.

Expert Utilization of Compiled Statistical and Non-Statistical Information

Up to this point, everything you've done has generated some type of information about the business. Upon reaching the profitability stage, you must exchange your "gatherer" status to that of a "composer." It's time now to review the information and statistics you've gathered, and compile them into a format that gives you some idea of current value, potential value, and realistic selling price. The use of a valuation expert may seem expensive at first, but once you have reached the price-setting stage and negotiations begin, the value set by a valuation expert is hard to refute. It is not unusual to receive eight or ten times the benefit compared to the cost of the valuation expert.

Determine the Best Method for Reaching Top Dollar on the Sell

Once again, take the information you've gathered but view it from a different angle. This time, look for any discrepancies and any unfinished or rough edges. Packaging your business for selling is no different from packaging your product for selling. The more appealing you make the packaging and presentation, the more likely the sale. Review your financials and make absolutely certain they present the cleanest, best image of your business value that is possible. Don't hesitate to show earnings; there's nothing more impressive and powerful than irrefutable earnings and profit. These are the golden jewels every buyer seeks in a purchase proposition. Perform a valuation analysis of the business. Run the EBIT figures, and make sure that your add-backs are not excessive and that you don't have a long list of one-time events. Review the non-financial pieces of information: market share, economic indicators, industry health, and the host of other value drivers for your business. Are the results in support of the sell? Do the answers to non-financial and value-driver questions indicate that your business is at the top? The answers to these questions should be a resounding "yes"; if that's the case, it indicates that it's a prime time to sell.

Evaluate Your Flexibility

When you package your business for selling, how flexible are you going to be when the buyer makes demands of staggered payouts, non-compete covenants, or a retainer on owner participation? You shouldn't expect to get the most from your business if you have no intention of bending on some of the requirements. Potential buyers feel more comfortable dealing with sellers who aren't afraid to stick around. They also are happier with a staggered buyout structure because they need less money up front and are often willing to give more for the total package price. This brings us to the next topic: choosing your buyer and market.

Choose Your Market and Your Buyer Carefully

In order to get top dollar for the business, you need a buyer who sees potential and value in acquiring the business. There is generally a certain segment of the market and certain types of buyers that see a business as more valuable than other members of the market or buyer types. Your responsibility lies in finding that market and that buyer. Sometimes, this is a matter of timing and being in the right place at the right time. But anyone can search and increase the possibility of receiving the best price possible by simply looking for the right individual or group in the right market.

Tie Up the Loose Ends

As we discussed in the review of the financials, tie up all loose ends, both actual and physical. Make absolutely certain that the physical location and facilities that you are offering for sale look the part. All areas of the facility should be well-kept and clean, equipment should be serviced and in top form, and any other key physical locations to be included in the sale should be checked also.

Know Your Buyer or Seller, as the Case May Be

We touched briefly on the subject of the buyer in the methods you should use to achieve top dollar. Here, we are making reference to your ability to gauge your buyer's wants, needs, and perceptions. The more you know about your buyer, the better equipped you are at the negotiation table and in reaching an agreeable price. Never underestimate your opponent. This principle applies to war, chess, and selling a business. The more you know about a potential buyer, the better equipped you are when it comes to making demands or concessions; structuring buyout deals or just plain knowing when to give and take is often dependent upon your knowledge of the individual across the table.

Be Flexible with the Deal Structure

This is one of the key issues at the negotiating table. Often, price is not the big issue. How to pay for the purchase and how to assure that the business will continue to thrive are key issues. If you are a seller and you aren't willing to make any concessions, you run a greater risk of losing the buyout opportunity; if you are already aware of the options you can live with, you give the impression that you are willing to work with the buyer to accomplish the sell and that you are an individual willing to work with a buyer. These are very important selling points; even if the buyer should decide not to exercise the flexibility issue, he or she may just need to know you were willing. There is another piece of this puzzle here, however, that you may need to work in your favor: the tax ramifications of an up-front cash buyout versus a structured two- to three-year buyout.

Perform Tax Planning

Here is where a great majority of your profits leave your possession and move into the hands of the Internal Revenue Service. You've spent years carefully building and mothering a business, waiting for the moment when you can sell, retire, and live a life of ease. Unfortunately, if you have not taken the time to carefully review the consequences of selling the business as it applies to your finances, you may not walk away with the retirement nest egg you think you should; however, with some forethought and planning, you might walk away with more than you thought. We're going to take a few paragraphs here to review all-cash deals versus structured buyouts versus earn-outs and provide you with some basic information that is at least a beginning for you and your CPA. The tax liability can sometimes be tremendous under one plan yet virtually non-existent in other plans. As we review each buyout option, we will discuss the issues that affect both buyer and seller, and you will need to apply that information to your individual situation to determine the tax liability you can expect to incur.

An All-Cash Deal

The seller demands the entire selling price in cash up front. This is really not the ideal way to sell a business; however, there are certain circumstances when it is the only way. Given a choice, I would suggest that you choose one of the other methods as the tax liability when the entire purchase price of the sale is received in a lump-sum settlement is much greater. The all-cash method requires that the buyer come up with the entire amount upon purchasing the business; not only does this mean the buyer risks the entire investment, but it also limits the amount of excess cash available for business operations.

The Structured-Buyout Option

It eases the strain for the buyer during initial operations and reduces the tax liability for the seller. How does the structured buyout work? There are many variations. One basic form requires the buyer to produce a certain percentage of the total purchase price during the closing of the deal and then the balance at a future specified date. Quite often, the seller is encouraged to remain with the business in order to ensure its success, and the new buyer doesn't feel quite so burdened with excessive business debt. Another variation of the structured buyout provides the seller with several alternate offers for the same business by the same buyer but at varying levels of purchase price. Say, for instance, the EBIT method has been used, and the multiple for a stock purchase is ten times EBIT; for half cash/half stock, the multiple used is nine times EBIT; for all cash up front, six times EBIT. You can see how a structured deal here would greatly increase the seller's profits.

The Earn-Out Option

In almost all of these deal structures, the owner remains with the business for several years following the sale in order to assure the business's continued success. The use of earn-outs provides not only a tax benefit to the seller, but it is also a way for the seller to share in the continued growth of the business. It reduces the buyer's risk of overpayment, reduces the cash required from the buyer at closing, helps to alleviate any uncertainty the buyer might have about the future success of the business, and protects the buyer if there was insufficient due diligence performed. This unique relationship, however, requires immeasurable trust between the buyer and the seller. There are other non-financial factors that play a part in the decision to use an earn-out option. Who is the beneficiary? In some cases, both parties receive some level of benefit such as in situations where the seller has been losing money, when the buyer has limited equity, when relationships are being transferred as in some sales and service companies, and when the business is introducing new products. These are all risky propositions, and earn-outs are used as an inducement to buy or sell, depending on your position.

These buyout and structured-deal topics will be covered extensively in Chapter 9: The Deal. However, you do need a basic understanding of the concepts that exist in choosing one particular method over the other and the potential repercussions, both financial and non-financial.

Converting Value Drivers to Dollar Value

If you've finished the valuation information found in Chapter 5, you should have an excellent idea of the value drivers that are found within your individual business; what you might not understand is how to convert those value drivers into a dollar benefit, known as deal drivers. The idea is quite simple yet may be very complex and difficult to carry out. Once you have determined what your value drivers are, you must compare the value drivers to the market segment and particular buyer you're trying to reach. The ability to detect the vantage point that makes the value driver financially valuable is the key. Suppose you're a regional business and you're trying to sell your product to a national buyer. If you approach the deal from the viewpoint of inadequacy—in other words, we have a small customer base; therefore, we aren't that valuable—you're going to leave lots of money on the table. Why? Suppose you approached it from this angle: While it's true we're only a regional business, we currently dominate 80 percent of that regional market. If you apply the same concept to the national market, your company stands to see a tremendous amount of growth in sales volume that will make your business worth much more. See? Find the angle and use it to your advantage. Using that approach, the business could easily be valued at the highest multiple possible and potentially bring millions more to the seller.

The goodwill factor has been a problem traditionally, but recent changes in tax regulations and a shift in lending perceptions about the value of goodwill have increased the value and the ability to deduct this asset. Does that have any effect on your ability to convert goodwill to dollars? It certainly does. Thanks to the new Financial Accounting Standards Board (FASB) rule, goodwill can be treated as a viable asset that, just like machinery and equipment, accounts for a certain percentage of the earnings of a business. The valuation of goodwill must be performed by an auditing firm that is certified to assess goodwill value; however, once confirmed, goodwill can add tremendous benefit—dollar benefit—to the profit of the buy/

sell agreement. I would not hesitate to have the goodwill of a business evaluated, as it can sometimes double the estimation of profitability of the business at the point of sale that would otherwise be left on the table.

Never Sell on Impulse

This advice should go without saying; but it seems that when small business owners are ready to sell, they're ready to sell. The number-one reason given for selling a small business is owner burnout. This condition within itself is conducive to impulse selling, but it doesn't net the seller top dollar for the business. Just as you should never impulse buy, you shouldn't impulse sell. Too many important variables remain unknown when you pull prices out of thin air. For the seller and the buyer, it is a risky and often doomed venture.

Don't Overvalue the Business

Sellers are often guilty of this. Your company's value is not based on the blood, sweat, and tears that you have spent in building the business. If that were the case, not one business owner would sell below several million. The valuation of the business must be based on irrefutable, hard evidence. Pricing the business too high can create several different yet equally undesirable situations. First, placing an unrealistic price on the business requires potential buyers to use greater leverage when purchasing it; this in turn can set up the new owner for failure. If you structure the buyout with earn-out options, you also stand to lose valuable profit. Second, businesses that are overvalued and remain on the market too long are often dismissed by potential buyers without so much as a peek at the selling memorandum. The network of intermediaries, buyers, sellers, and merger and acquisition (M&A) specialists that normally promote businesses works much like a grapevine or gossip. Once a business has become old news, has exceeded the normal sale time, and has developed a tarnished image, very few buyers are eager to approach the seller.

Have a Valuation Specialist Perform a Valuation of Your Business

It may cost a little money up front, but when complete, you and everyone else can feel confident that the price placed on the business is an accurate assessment of its worth. You stand to profit much sooner with realistic profit levels available.

This chapter has covered almost every possible issue that can affect profitability once the other responsibilities of the sell-preparation process have been met. These issues are of key importance to the seller's or buyer's personal input, negotiating power, and satisfaction with the final deal. You must take an active role in the negotiating and deal-making process; understanding how to perform those duties and understanding the boundaries of the deal limits allows you to be a better negotiator, and you can potentially walk away with more money.

CASE STUDY

H & H Enterprises is a jointly owned-and-operated husband-and-wife business that was formed simply out of necessity, opportunity, and youth. My wife and I were young, expecting our first child, and we needed extra income. I am a trained machinist, and my wife has a high school education. Thanks to the fact that my mother owned a restaurant, I had worked in food service and catering for several years prior to receiving my machinist's certificate. We capitalized on our contacts and experience.

Contact Information: Heath and Haley Aldridge
12657 Charles Taylor Rd.
Vance, AL 35490

The need for extra income is the reason my wife and I started our own business. We didn't really have much choice as to what type of business we could start. We had no other educational options, and no other work experience to draw upon. I had worked previously in the restaurant/catering industry, and my wife was very dedicated and committed to our venture. Add the fact that we had catering contacts, and it was an obvious choice.

We have had the opportunity to pull together, to work together, and become even closer as a family. Starting the business has also enabled my wife and me to be independent of our families and to provide the needed income on our own. Goodwill and customer loyalty definitely adds value to our business.

On the downside, it's hard work with long hours. Financially, we struggled from the initial lack of a payday while we paid for the necessary equipment. Although this was a short period of time, we were in real need of extra income. We borrowed money from my mom. Today, however, we have added to our economic value, and we use an accountant for our business recordkeeping.

I'd absolutely recommend starting a business to others. Although we're very young, I can see the tremendous advantage of owning and operating a successful business.

CHAPTER 7

THE
CAPITAL AND
FINANCING OPTIONS

Key issues:

- *Creditors and Lenders*
- *Owner/Seller Financing*
- *Capital Investment*
- *Venture Capitalists and Angel Investors*
- *Government Guarantees/SBA Funding*

FINANCING OPTIONS

We've now reached one of the really important parts of the entire process; after all, there will be no buy or sell transaction if there is no funding. There are just two basic ways to fund the business deal: equity or debt. Equity, of course, is your personal investment in the business. The debt is any capital you secure based on personal guarantees or pledging of assets that is used for the purchase of the business. The debt you secure can come from several different lending sources, and the more common ones are listed below and will be discussed in some detail. Let me take a moment to remind you that if you've put together your team of advisors and acquisition specialists, your banker or financier is the go-to guy at this juncture. He or she is very familiar (or should be) with the many different approaches to raising the necessary capital.

In Chapters 1 and 2 you evaluated your business profile and established your buying and selling criteria; some of those questions concerned your resources and level of willing commitment. Here in Chapter 7 we'll discuss how you go about securing the additional resources (funding and capital) that you will need.

You need to know what capital structure is and you need to understand how it works because you must be able to convert the information mentally as you examine a balance sheet. Capital structure refers to the assets and liabilities of the business. There are three sources of capital: creditors, lenders, and owners. We're going to discuss those in the next few paragraphs, but how does this convert to your business information found on the balance sheet?

1. Owner's investment is known as equity.

2. Creditor's investment is known as a current liability (accounts payable).

3. Lender's investment is known as long-term debt.

To see how it looks on a charted diagram, see Figure 7.1.

Figure 7.1

ASSETS	LIABILITIES	SOURCES OF CAPITAL
Current Assets Working Capital	Current Liabilities Short-Term Debt	Creditors
Tangible Assets	Long-Term Debt	Lenders
Intangible Assets	Shareholders' Equity	Owners

This is the way that capital is normally and ideally structured, with the changes in long-term debt and shareholders' equity becoming more equity than debt as the business is paid for.

If you use the balance sheet of a business to prepare a diagram such as the one shown above, you can more accurately determine your position when approaching lending institutions for financing. If the long-term debt is much greater than the owner equity and you're proposing to further stretch the debt of the business, don't look for a welcome reception at a traditional lending institution. Small companies may vary somewhat from the diagram but not greatly; and regardless of the size of the business, lending standards will not vary drastically. The diagram is also an excellent way to determine where you are as an owner when assessing your ability to borrow additional funds.

CREDITORS AND LENDERS

Lending Institutions

This normally equates to the banking industry for many of us; and as we cover lending institutions in this chapter, that is the intended industry. Some 90 percent of all business purchases include some form of seller financing, but there is also a tremendous percentage of purchases that include traditional bank business loans. What do banks require when you request business loans? A better question at this point might be how do you prepare to request a business loan? There are some really important issues to address when preparing to seek capital for a business purchase, and if you're going the way of the banking industry, here's what you need to know:

1. Choose a banker, not a bank; it's the banker you'll deal with.

2. Anticipate the basic questions: How much do you need, for how long, for what use, and how will you repay the loan?

3. Review your credit history and keep it clean with at least a 675–700 score.

4. Understand the traditional methods for lending money using the balance sheet, the cash flow, and the business assets.

5. Know how banks determine worthiness when lending, also known as the six C's of lending: *Character, cash flow, capital, collateral, condition, and capacity.*

   a) Character: Leads to a long-term relationship

   b) Cash flow: Ensures repayment

   c) Capital: Makes running the business possible

   d) Collateral: Covers any shortfall in the debt to equity

e) Condition: Determines lender's tolerance of risk

f) Capacity: Predicts ability to earn more money

When making the effort to obtain a bank loan, be prepared to inform the bank as to how you intend to run the business; provide the banker with the key essentials that outline how the business operates and what financial controls are in place to assure smooth business operations. Describe the business product or service and the manner in which it is marketed; give fairly detailed information about the company's management and any information about management personnel's background that will make an important contribution to the business success. Be prepared to answer specific and pointed questions about your intentions for the capital: how you are going to spend it, how you will repay the loan and when. Be prepared to make a presentation of the business financials, generally put together in a small handout. The financial presentation should provide the basic financials of the business, the projected increase in revenue if applicable, and an analysis of profitability. The best choice is to put together a formal business plan. Many lending institutions don't actually require one, but it makes a great first impression and also lets the lender know you've given your proposal serious thought and research. The business plan and the necessary content will be covered toward the end of the chapter. The seller's willingness to remain as a consultant is a tremendous inducement for the bank or lending institution when considering the request for financing and capital. Quite often, it can be the make-or-break issue when obtaining a loan. The lending institution has a low risk tolerance traditionally; and if the seller is willing to remain available as a consultant, this assures the bank that the same knowledge that built a successful business is available to help maintain that success.

If you're asked to provide a personal guarantee for the loan, are you prepared to do so? Since the banker's objective is different from yours, the lending institution will normally ask for one. If you aren't prepared to oblige, here are some alternative methods for dealing with this requirement:

1. Shop available lending institutions. Allowing lenders to compete for your business will provide you with some leverage concerning the loan parameters, one of which may be that you're seeking funding that doesn't require a personal guarantee. It may affect the amount you're able to secure, but you just might succeed.

2. If you are required to sign the loan with a personal guarantee, establish the limits for release. In other words, pin down the lending institution as to when they will release you from the guarantee.

3. Don't sign personal guarantees that say "joint and several guarantee" because this allows the bank to collect from both the business and you, the guarantor, at the same time. Have them prepare the paperwork to include an indemnification guarantee, which simply means that the bank cannot collect from the personal guarantor until the business fails to pay its obligations.

4. Have an agreement drawn up that releases you at a certain level of payoff on the note; generally, lending institutions will not allow release for anything higher than 50 percent.

5. Propose to share the personal guarantee with the other shareholders if the business is operating as a

corporation. Although corporations are organized to protect the shareholders from unlimited liability, you can draw up an agreement that allows for personal guarantee of their share percentage.

6. Add a stipulation to the personal guarantee that doesn't allow the guarantee to become effective until the business has missed "x" number of payments.

When the bank or lending institution begins a review of your proposal, what are the key issues you should have presented and put together? Here's the major rundown:

Certain lenders make certain size loans. Know the bread-and-butter loan size for the lender you approach. This means you need to research the vast majority of the loans the proposed lender makes. What size are they? Lenders are just like people. They're much more comfortable making loans they are familiar with; stay within the appropriate range.

Since staying within a comfort zone is best, even with lenders, put together a business plan that contains all the elements the lending institution will look for when evaluating your loan request. Have your financials, a clearly defined objective, a strategic plan that will be feasible, and a proposed repayment plan that will work even with a worst-case scenario.

The lender will examine the balance sheet and financials of the business closely. If the business is highly leveraged, you will probably be required to commit a larger amount of capital. If not, and the balance sheet and financials look good, a personal guarantee may be optional. Lending institutions loan money on accounts receivables, inventory, and machinery and equipment; sometimes, the lending institution will require periodic audits of cash flow and income statements to provide verification that the operation is profitable.

When the lending institution takes a look at you, the individual, here is what they look for: Does the creditor have a good reputation, character, and business background? Has the creditor carved out a niche for him or herself in this particular field? If the answers here are satisfactory, the lending institution can begin to feel comfortable about extending the credit. This issue is crucial to obtaining funds. If you're inexperienced in the area, you have no prior business background, and you have no reputation within the business community, I wouldn't hold out very much hope of obtaining a loan through a traditional lending institution. Don't forget, however, that part of your job is to sell yourself and your proposal. If all the variables are in place, be persistent. It will usually pay off with a loan from the lending institution.

Accounts Receivable and Inventory Lenders

Also known as factoring, these lenders will advance the business money based on a percentage of outstanding accounts receivable or in-house inventory levels. These alternative loan options are not really recommended for healthy businesses since there are other, more stable options that will cost the business less in the long run.

Unsecured Lenders

These are banks and other lending institutions that will make loans based on the cash flow of a company: There are five key criteria that these lending institutions rely on to determine unsecured lending:

1. The amount of cash flow generated by the business.

2. The type of available collateral.

3. The credit of the borrowers.

4. The debt-to-equity ratio of the business.

5. The financial strength of the borrowers.

These loans are generally for business owners already in business who need capital funding for only a short while or due to seasonal workload. The recipients of these loans are highly scrutinized, and many small business buyers simply are not candidates.

OWNER/SELLER FINANCING

Seller-Financed Mortgages

Seller-financed mortgages make up approximately 90 percent of all small business purchases. Quite often, the seller financing is a result of the negotiation process and can serve to assure potential sellers some level of continued contact with a business and the buyer the necessary capital to close the deal. This type of financing is so prevalent among small business buy-and-sell transactions that I am devoting several pages to the examination of options and creative ways a buyer and seller can accommodate one another through the use of seller financing. There are as many ways to use this option as there are buyers and sellers. The use of structured buyout deals, earn-out options, and seller retention of business interest are the most popular, but they are not the only methods for completing the sale of a business. The reason seller-financed mortgages are so popular with small businesses is that all too often traditional lending institutions will not lend the necessary amount of capital to bridge the gap between the buyer's personal investment and the seller's asking price. Goodwill is not as easily established and verified when dealing with small businesses, and many of the venture capitalists are simply not in the market for small, privately held businesses. The best alternative: seller financing.

When you are negotiating the buyout deal structure and seller financing is going to be considered for part of the buyout deal, bear in mind the following issues:

1. If the seller is willing to provide seller financing, how much up-front cash will be required?

2. Will a personal guarantee for the balance be required, or will the assets of the business be used as collateral?

3. If the assets are used as collateral, will a second lien and a backseat to other creditors or lenders be acceptable?

4. Will the seller consider the earn-out/buyout options that tie eventual payment to the performance of the business?

5. If the earn-out option will be considered, will the seller want to remain involved with the business on some level? For how long?

6. What are the tax and income considerations of the seller? Will the buyout require that the seller pay a tremendous amount of tax for capital gains?

7. If so, would the seller consider receiving the financing for non-compete agreements, an employment contract, or consulting fees?

All of these questions are plausible, credible questions if seller financing is an option, and many of these questions you will need to explore during negotiations and deal structuring. Some situations work to the buyer's benefit, some to the seller, and some benefit both parties. Those are the choices you hope to make, those of mutual benefit.

Structured buyouts often include a promissory note to the seller to be paid at a later date, assuming the business remains operational and profitable. Although on the surface this seems a bit risky, if the seller has been upfront concerning non-financial business issues and the buyer is well qualified to operate a small business, the likelihood of success and eventual receipt of the promissory note amount are great. Other spinoffs on this particular arrangement include the seller's continued input on a contractual basis. As a seller, there is more assurance of success and eventual receipt of the final payout if you are still an active participant in the business in a much smaller way. You are still available to help the new owner transition into the business and hopefully minimize mistakes that create losses, but you are not ultimately responsible for operations.

Earn-outs are a better deal for the buyer than for the seller unless the buyer and seller have a lot of confidence in each other and have a trusting relationship. Ultimately, the seller is at the buyer's mercy; the seller must depend on the buyer to accurately report earnings in order to adequately assess the earn-out amount if based on percentages; if not, accuracy is simply necessary for a yes or no situation. Yes, we made money, so here is yours; or no, we didn't make money, so you don't get the earn-out pay.

CAPITAL INVESTMENT

Personal Investment or Owner Equity

As I stated in an earlier section, you must be willing to commit personal resources to the success of this venture; and quite frankly, any institution you contact for funding will ask you what portion of the purchase price you are going to cover with personal investment. During your self-analysis and the determination of your search criteria, you should have addressed this issue and at this juncture be prepared to anticipate these questions. Your plan should include your proposed level of investment and personal contribution to the operation and guarantee of success to the business. There is also the option of equity investors that will be discussed in the financing options section next.

Equity financing is a critical component of the deal structure. When you begin the process of purchasing a business, you are making an investment of your time; before the purchase is complete, it will require an investment of equity or capital. If you're not prepared for this, you shouldn't begin the process. Why is an equity or capital investment necessary? There are several good reasons that have nothing to do with your level of commitment. One, it increases the asset value of the business immediately. Two, there is no debt to be repaid and no interest on the debt; therefore, your break-even analysis doesn't have to cover additional monthly payments. Three, there is no need to tie up existing company assets as collateral. Who provides equity or capital investment and are there any disadvantages? Let's answer one question at a time.

There are individuals willing to provide equity or capital investment for your business purchase. You might choose to be one of those individuals. These types of investors are a spin-off of the venture capitalists with one exception: they generally choose less risk in favor of more stable companies. The trade off, of course, is less of a profit on their return. However, the equity investors are a valuable option, especially if you have access to private citizens who are investment savvy with cash to invest. The drawback with the use of other individuals is that they require a return on their investment, also known as ROI. It is generally higher than the prime interest rate because their risk is greater. Second, the higher ROI means that the equity investment is more expensive than financed debt. Third, the equity investor becomes a kind of silent partner — silent if things go well; if not, loud and obnoxious at times. Where do you look for equity investment? Business associates, friends, relatives, and private investors or venture capitalists/companies. How can you determine which source of funding to use, equity or financed debt? There is a general nine-factor evaluation that can be performed to answer this question.

1. Determine if your investors have additional cash that can be invested at a future date should the need arise, especially if it will be needed for emergency operating cash. If the answer is no, maybe you should look to another individual or an alternative form of financing.

2. If you're buying stocks and all the liabilities that go with a stock purchase, the potential legal issues could have a significant impact on your decision. Seek the

advice of an attorney; if it looks too risky, it is.

3. Determine the number of investors you will need. Determine the level of investment you're seeking from each investor. It might or might not be a feasible proposition.

4. Determine how much control you're comfortable relinquishing should you take on equity investors; if you're not at ease with the possibility of allowing investors to control your business, seek other sources of funding.

5. Consider your investor's desired rate of return. Would the trade off for debt financing with a lower payout of interest versus the non-debt use of equity with a high rate of return be a better choice?

6. What are the complications and repercussions if the business should fail? If your equity investors are friends and family, the personal and emotional problems that a failure could cause might not be worth the use of the equity. There have been many instances of failure with the use of friends' and relatives' money that drove the entrepreneurs involved into deep depressions with excessive guilt. Do you have any doubts about the success of the venture? If so, seek other funding.

7. Often, the better choice when seeking equity investors is to approach the sophisticated, professional investor. Skip family and friends. Choose individuals who are well aware of the risks involved.

8. If you already have potential investors, ask for contacts. People who are equity investors generally have business contacts who are also equity investors.

9. If you do make the decision to go with equity investors, choose investors with credibility and excellent reputations. That factor alone will induce others to join you.

VENTURE CAPITALISTS AND ANGEL INVESTORS

Venture capitalists and venture capital companies are at the top of the list because they are often the most inclined to take risks. The venture capitalists don't loan you money; they invest money in your venture or business. They will extract a profit on that investment over the course of no more than a ten-year commitment, and the profit levels are substantially higher than the interest rate you will receive at a formal lending institution. But the tradeoff is often worth the loss of profit in that if you are a higher-than-normal lending risk, you generally aren't an excessive risk for the venture capitalists.

There are four types of venture capital investing entities: independent private venture capital firms, small business investment companies, minority enterprise small business investment companies, and venture capital subsidiaries of large financial institutions and industrial corporations. Each one and their general investing requirements will be discussed in the following paragraphs.

Independent Private Venture Capital Firms

These are privately held firms or organizations that invest private funds in a business for a return on investment in the neighborhood of 20 to 30 percent, or match equity for a lesser ROI, or sometimes take an active role in the management of the business for a lesser ROI. It is through this group that we have come to use the term angel investors: venture capital investors who are willing to risk capital investment and extend their expertise in certain areas in order to increase the business's likelihood of success. If you're looking to secure this type of investment, the best place to start will be with your financial advisor and the Internet. There are many reputable firms and individuals that have business listings on the Web, and if your financial advisor doesn't have anyone to recommend, check out the Web sites and then check the Better Business Bureau.

Small Business Investment Companies

These are a type of venture capitalist except that they often will require not a part of the business as venture capitalists do, but a greater return on their investment than the traditional lending institutions. They are willing to assume more risk, and this equates to a greater possibility of receiving the necessary capital for the buyer; but they expect a greater return than the 6 to 8 percent interest the traditional lenders will require. The Small Business Administration has formed and continues to work with small business investment companies to provide the necessary funding for many rural and economically depressed areas. In order to learn more about these programs, check out the SBA at **www.sba.gov**.

Minority Enterprise Small Business Investment Companies

This type of investing is a spin-off from the SBIC; it serves, however, only the minority business environment. The minority small business obstacles can be tremendous, and thanks to a joint effort between private and government individuals and entities, these MESBICs were formed to serve minority small business prospects.

Venture Capital Subsidiaries of Large Financial Institutions

These are branches of traditional lending institutions that are more regulated and harder to acquire capital from. Many of the large financial institutions are capitalizing on the venture capital market by funding small business enterprises through a subsidiary that is funded in part by institutional funds and in part by private funding. This type of venture-capital investment will yield the investors a much higher rate of return but also with a higher ratio of risk.

What are venture capitalists really doing when they invest in a business? They're really investing in the potential that exists. The value of the business in its current condition is not what they are investing in. They are investing in the faith that the business venture will pay off. For this reason, it is up to you to make the best case possible when seeking venture capital. When applying for traditional funding, the lender asks for certain information that provides a solid base in the event that you fail. In other words, they're not as concerned with your success as your failure. With venture-capital investors, the focus is shifted to your potential success, not your current value. Venture capitalists are interested in your intangibles as well as your tangibles: your level of experience, determination, and motivation. Then they will explore location, demographics, and other value-driven information. If your need for capital borders on the edge of acceptable to traditional lenders, venture capitalists may be your best option.

Government Guarantees/SBA Funding

SBA-secured loans are government-guaranteed business loans. The government is not the direct lender, simply a guarantor on the loan with the business. The banks and other lending institutions are more agreeable to loaning businesses money if there is a government guarantee on the return. The Small Business Administration has grown dramatically over the last couple of decades as the environment in the United States has encouraged small business growth. The government mandates that the departments awarding contracts to individual businesses will set aside so much of the budget for contracted work to small business. This money is set aside even if the product or service comes at a higher price. What is asked for in return for government guarantees and SBA-approved funding? Business plans and lots of government paperwork.

THE BUSINESS PLAN

Just as we have emphasized the importance of planning during the initial process of buying and selling businesses, potential investors, lenders, and venture capitalists will need some documentation that provides information about your intentions once you acquire the business. This is the purpose of the business plan; and one that is properly constructed will take several months to put together. You could hope for the existence of a previous business plan to use as a base for one that will suit your purpose. At any rate, you should understand the essential elements of the business plan and how to acquire the information you will need to complete it. The following paragraphs briefly detail the business plan by major sections and provide you with suggested sources for the information you will need.

The executive summary provides an overview of your objectives, mission, and perceived keys to success. This is called an executive summary for a reason; keep it concise, clear, and very professional. Your statements here will introduce your ideas to prospects, and you want the first impression to be a devastatingly effective one.

The company summary provides detailed information concerning the company ownership, location, facilities, proposed changes, and forecasted effect. The company-ownership section will explain exactly that—how will the business be owned? Will it be an S corporation, a proprietorship, or a partnership? Location and facility requires physical address information, the size and location of your business or proposed business, and any pertinent facts about the location and size that would need to be furnished should the funding be received. It does not need too much detail, just enough to give a clear picture. The proposed changes and forecasted effect are your real opportunities to sell the idea. In these discussions, make sure that you have given much thought and research to your proposal so that you can accurately make it and subsequently forecast the expected benefit.

The strategy summary provides an overview of the strategies used to maintain market share and expand and grow the market share, any anticipated ventures into new markets, and marketing campaigns. You will be expected to answer some tough questions here such as how you propose to gain entry into a market you're not already in, what is your competitive advantage, what is your relevant experience, and how will you target and increase your market? The answers here will require work on your part; but if the business is worth starting, it's worth some startup research and legwork.

The management summary will list management team members and any relevant information such as experience, education, and achievements, management strengths and weaknesses, and any other key personnel. You are the seller here! This is your chance to motivate your potential lenders, investors; whomever you may be pitching your idea to. If you're a successful entrepreneur already, you have verifiable credentials and years of on-the-job training. What if you're not? Sit down with your résumé, and make the most of it. Whatever you're seeking funding for, make sure you have experience; if you don't, make sure your management team does. No one is going to invest in someone who doesn't know what he or she is doing in an industry or has no previous background in that field.

The financial summary provides detailed information about the company's previous operating information and should include any perceived changes in sales forecasts, operational expenses, productivity levels, and the dollar impact, as well as any economic indicators that would affect the business financials. The most recent financial statements would also be included in this section of the business plan.

The financial summary should also include a detailed listing of the business's accounts receivables and payables; equipment and machinery; real estate, to include the estimated fair market value (with appraisals if necessary); and any financial statements for the borrowers and guarantors. In addition to the financial summary information, many investors and lending institutions will request supporting documentation for the information provided in the financial summary section. What are these documents? If you're seeking capital for a franchise business, your approach will be a little different, and that's basically for another book!

Supporting documents will include financial statements for the last three years plus a current year-to-date statement; a breakdown of the accounts receivables and inventory; a list of machinery, equipment, and real estate that indicates estimated values including appraisals if necessary; a description of the management team; financial projections; a complete description of what the funds will be used for; and personal financial statements of the borrowers and guarantors.

CASE STUDY

Kathy's Ink is an administrative/temp service that provides needed office and administrative service on a contract basis. The business was started as a result of the owner's layoff from a local manufacturing facility, and the need for temporary administrative help in the community.

Contact Information: Kathy Williams
1291 12th St.
Vernon, AL 35592

I started Kathy's Ink to provide income for my family. Administrative and office tasks were all I knew how to do, and it was a much-needed service in our community. My knowledge of the work, the industry, and my commitment to work excellence have all been important in starting my business.

It's been great operating my own business, and having the opportunity to determine when and how long I work. Additionally, the income has been as good, if not better, than that of my previous job, and I enjoy the work.

Starting out, it was difficult at times to build my reputation and get enough work. Financially, I had to acquire the needed startup capital to purchase the equipment, so I borrowed the money from my bank against money in savings. Today, I feel as though Kathy's Ink has contributed economic value to the community and to the economy.

I would recommend starting a business to others. I think it's great to own your business, set goals and objectives, and know that you're only limited by your own desires and work commitment.

PART III:

THE
REALIZATION

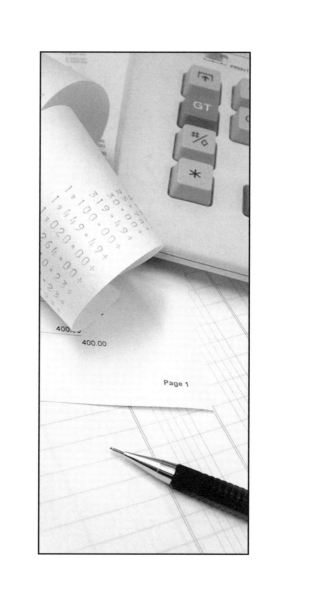

CHAPTER 8

THE NEW BEGINNING: BUSINESS ORGANIZATION, LEGAL DOCUMENTS, AND TAX ISSUES

The key issues addressed in Chapter 8 are the following:

- *Legal Issues*
- *Forms of Organization*
- *Business Licenses*
- *Federal and State Employer Requirements*
- *Tax Issues*
- *Tax Planning*

LEGAL ISSUES

The legal documentation that will be needed will be determined by the legal organization of the business, the particulars of the structured buyout, the representations and warranties, and the covenants executed during the closing. As a matter of course and good sense, each party should be represented with legal counsel during the course of the negotiations, the construction of the buy/sell agreement, and the closing and execution of these documents.

There are so many legal issues that concern the buyer and seller during this process that devoting one chapter to address those issues seemed in order. From business organization options to the performance of due diligence, the legal obligations and consequences to the buyer and seller are issues that absolutely must be addressed.

As a buyer, will you be responsible for the existing legal contracts and liabilities of the seller? Answers to questions like this lie in the way you structure the buyout and the decisions you make about organizing your new business. In addressing the legal issues at hand, let's start with some of the most obvious and work our way through the others that will probably confront you before you're able to close the deal.

Asset versus stock is a huge issue during the legal considerations and tax negotiations. If you purchase the assets of a business, you are only purchasing an object; you do not purchase any prior liens, liabilities, obligations, etc. If you purchase the stock of a corporation, you purchase everything about that business. So why isn't every deal structured as an asset purchase? Because of capital-gains issues, tax liability, and the fact that the vast majority of small businesses aren't corporations but sole proprietorships, and the only option available is to purchase the assets. The difference between the asset value and the actual price paid is attributable to what's known as goodwill, and only recently has a business been able to amortize and deduct the goodwill asset of a business; prior to that option, buyers and sellers increased the fair-market-value price of the assets and closed the deal. The disadvantage there?

In most cases, there is a capital-gains tax that must be paid by the seller, and a use tax that will be paid by the purchaser that is greater than the actual value of the assets. Navigating these waters can be very difficult; and if you're not extremely careful, you'll cost yourself and your business lots of money. Seek the advice of legal counsel.

FORMS OF BUSINESS ORGANIZATION

Your choice of organization has extreme importance during the buy/sell arrangements, and your choices here will affect your future tax liability and legal obligations. When you're selling a business, if it is incorporated and you must seek the approval of other stockholders, it can make the process a long and somewhat arduous one, especially if some of the stockholders don't want to sell. If you're organizing a new business, you will basically have three choices, as there are three basic forms of organization: sole proprietorship, corporation, and partnership.

The sole proprietorship is the simplest of all three forms, as there is no legal documentation to complete other than purchasing a business license in the locality in which you operate. It is owned by a single individual and controlled by that individual. You are personally liable for all the debts, liabilities, and business transactions. This is where the disadvantages begin to outweigh the advantages. Your business is reliant upon you for net worth and raising capital. If you should experience financial troubles, so will your business and vice versa.

Partnerships can be formed in two ways: general partnerships and limited partnerships; either choice is formed with little formality and exists when two people are engaged in a venture for profit. You can choose to establish written articles of partnership or your arrangement can be only an oral agreement. Each partner shares equally in the profit, loss, and liabilities of the business. Each partner has equal control over the operation and management of the business. In a limited partnership, you must file a limited partnership certificate; and partners are limited to the extent of their investment. This type of arrangement is formed when you have investors who wish to provide monetary support and nothing more. This type of arrangement will generally cost more than forming a corporation, and often the corporate choice is the most desirable one when you have more than one investor and the sole-proprietorship choice is not an option.

Corporations follow a specific code of requirements and legal documentation, but when complete, you, the shareholder, are only liable to the extent of your investment; you're not personally liable for the actions of the corporation. If you choose to do so, you can sell your shares of the corporation. There are two different forms of incorporation: S and C; the C corporations are more complicated than the S chapter, but if you're going to be a large company with public investors and shareholders, this will be your only option. If a company has fewer than 35 investors, there are no non-resident aliens as shareholders, it is a domestic corporation, and it is not a subsidiary of another corporation, the S chapter filing is the best choice: There is no double taxation of profit, and it works extremely well for small businesses.

Non-compete clauses are requested in order to prevent a former business owner from moving a few hundred feet up the road and opening for business again. As a new owner, you want to make sure you're not competing with a previous successful owner for customers that have a loyalty to him or her. Generally, when individuals sell small businesses, it is because there has been a change in mindset. They are aging and choose to retire, or they can find no viable replacement candidate among family members. If this is the case, they generally do not choose to start again and open a competing business.

Customer/Vendor contracts in existence and made a part of the buy/sell agreement will have legal and financial ramifications for the new owner. This affects your customer accounts, your accounts receivables, and sometimes any existing use of contract or freelance labor. Vendors and customers acquired during the buy/sell transaction are generally quite receptive to new owners provided there are no pre-existing issues. You should not neglect to investigate any customers and vendors, especially large accounts, to ascertain that there are no existing legal issues or pending litigation

When choosing a form of business, please take the time to consider the following issues:

1. Tax treatment of the entity, the owners, and the employees.

2. The business organization versus management organization.

3. The number of owners/shareholders.

4. The degree of liability desired by the owners/ shareholders.

5. The legal requirements of each form of business.

6. The capital needed for investment and methods of raising capital.

7. The legal regulations relating to the dissolution or termination of the entity.

8. The ease of organization.

9. The time required to organize the business form.

10. The recordkeeping and reporting requirements.

11. The cost of legal, professional, and advisory personnel.

BUSINESS LICENSES

There is not a lot of information to cover in this section except that it bears mentioning because as a new business owner, you may or may not be familiar with all the business licensing you may be required to obtain. Make sure that you check with your local, county, and state government entities. Generally, all businesses will need to obtain a local business license; and depending upon your industry and scope of operation, you may need additional licensing.

FEDERAL AND STATE EMPLOYER REQUIREMENTS

One of the most important terms you will need to be familiar with is the FEIN. The FEIN, or the Federal Employer Identification Number, is necessary if your business has employees. If you are an individual operating a business as a sole proprietor without employees or partners or without the need to incorporate, then you are not required to apply for an FEIN. Most of the other forms of business organization will require the use of an FEIN. These forms include corporations, estates, trusts, multiple businesses operated by a single individual, or a sole proprietor subject to a bankruptcy proceeding. The application process requires that you complete the form SS-4; all the necessary instructions, forms, and most frequently asked questions can be accessed via the Internet at **www.irs.gov**, or hard copies may be obtained at your local IRS office. The IRS Web site also gives detailed information concerning the location of your local IRS office. Currently, you can apply for an FEIN with hard copy mailed or faxed to the IRS or via the Internet and electronically submitted. Keep in mind, the FEIN is a federal number, and there will also be a need to contact your state and possibly local government entity to obtain employer withholding account numbers for their purposes also.

TAX ISSUES

If capital gains and capital investments sound confusing, take just a minute to read what we're actually saying. When you purchase a business or invest your money in a business, you have a capital investment. Over years and with continued success, the capital investment grows. Should you decide to sell that business and you receive $10,000 more than you originally invested, you have a capital gain. The IRS taxes capital gains but at a much lower rate than on income that is classified as regular income. This perspective is from the seller's point of view. Now let's look at it from the buyer's point of view:

Any monies invested as a capital investment aren't expensed; they're depreciated. There is one exception known as Section 179 expense, but it's limited. If you purchase the stock of a business, you also purchase the liability, and if there is no delay in partial payment, you must cough up all the money at the time of the buy/sell closing. Any payments that can be expensed such as earn-out or buyout payments that are paid directly to the seller as a condition of projected sales is an expense that decreases profits and therefore decreases tax liability.

Profit and loss and retained earnings affect your bottom line at the end of the year and, therefore, affect your tax liability. Once again, if any part of the buy/sell agreement can be structured as a staggered payout in the form of consulting agreements, earn-outs, and/or buyouts, that money can be expensed and reduce the profit and the tax liability.

Consulting agreements, earn-outs, and structured buyouts are key issues at the negotiating table. Often, price is not the big issue. How to pay for the purchase and assure that the business continues to thrive are key issues. If you are a seller and you aren't willing to make any concessions, you run a greater risk of losing the buyout opportunity; if you are already aware of the options you can live with, you give the buyer the impression that you are willing to work with the buyer to accomplish the sell and that you are an individual willing to work with a buyer. There is another piece of this puzzle here, however, that you may need to work in your favor: the tax ramifications of an up-front cash buyout versus a structured two- to three-year buyout. The tax liability can sometimes be tremendous under one plan yet virtually nonexistent in other plans. As we review each buyout option again, we will discuss the issues that affect both buyer and seller, and you will need to apply that information to your individual situation to determine the tax liability you can expect to incur.

An all-cash deal takes place when the seller demands the entire selling price in cash up front. This is really not the ideal way to sell a business; however, there are certain circumstances under which it is the only way. Given a choice, I would suggest that you choose one of the other methods; the tax liability when the entire purchase price of the sale is received in a lump-sum settlement is much greater. The all-cash method requires that the buyer come up with the entire amount upon purchasing the business; not only does this mean the buyer risks the entire investment, but it also limits the amount of excess cash available for business operations.

The structured buyout option is the most popular method used today. It eases the strain for the buyer during initial operations and reduces the tax liability for the seller. How does the structured buyout work? There are many variations. One basic form requires the buyer to produce a certain percentage of the total purchase price during the closing of the deal and then the balance at a future specified date. Quite often, the seller is encouraged to remain with the business in order to ensure its success, and the new buyer doesn't feel quite so burdened with excessive business debt. Another variation of the structured buyout provides the seller with several alternative offers for the same business by the same buyer but at varying levels of purchase price. Say, for instance, the EBIT method has been used, and the multiple for a stock purchase is ten times EBIT for half cash/half stock, the multiple used is nine times EBIT; for all cash up front, six times EBIT. You can see how a structured deal here would greatly increase the seller's profits

The earn-out option works similarly to the buyout option except that it ties the future payment of monies to the future performance of the business. In almost all of these particular deal structures, the owner remains with the business for several years following the sell in order to assure the business's continued success. The use of earn-outs provides not only a tax-liability benefit to the seller but it is also a way for the seller to share in the continued growth of the business. It reduces the buyer's risk of overpayment and reduces the buyer's cash at closing. It helps to alleviate any uncertainty the buyer might have about the future success of the business, and it protects the buyer if there was insufficient due diligence performed. This unique relationship, however, requires immeasurable trust between the buyer and the seller. There are other non-financial factors that play a part in the decision to use an earn-out option. Who is the beneficiary? In some cases, both parties receive some level of benefit such as when the seller has been losing money; when the buyer has limited equity, when relationships are being transferred in sales or service companies, or when the business is introducing new products. These are all risky propositions, and earn-outs are used as an inducement to buy or sell, depending on your position.

PERFORM TAX PLANNING

This is the point where most of your profits leave your possession and move into the hands of the Internal Revenue Service. You've spent years carefully building and promoting a business, waiting for the moment when you can sell, retire, and live a life of ease. Unfortunately, if you've not taken the time to carefully review the consequences of the sale of the business as it applies to your finances, you may not walk away with the retirement nest egg you think you should; however, with some forethought and planning, you might walk away with more than you thought.

All of these issues should be thoroughly examined prior to composing the letter of intent because this pre-contractual written instrument defines the preliminary understandings of the parties involved who are about to undertake and engage in contractual and binding negotiations. A complete and thorough understanding of the legal and tax implications as well as any of the purchasing options that might have legal and tax implications must be accomplished beforehand.

Chapter 9 begins with the information necessary for successful negotiations, and the letter of intent is the initial document used to form the basis for negotiations.

CASE STUDY

Nanny's Kids, Inc. is a daycare center that operates in a small rural community and provides the only commercial daycare available within a 20-mile radius. The center began operations in the family home, and after many years of hard work and building a reputation, the daycare is now in a commercial building, with an ever-increasing, bustling bunch of kids.

> *Contact Information: Sheila Gilpin*
> *12662 Hwy 96*
> *Millport, AL 35576*

Because I needed a full-time job and wanted to stay at home with my children, I started my own daycare business, Nanny's Kids, Inc. I had many years of care-giving experience and lots of commitment and dedication. I also wanted to be a stay-at-home mom and still provide my family with additional income. Daycare seemed like an excellent solution.

It's been great getting to work with children and to watch them as they grow and develop. My own family has been blessed with "adopted" brothers and sisters. Financially, the additional income has been a big advantage. However, in the beginning, the money I needed to provide the kind of resources I wanted to furnish for the children sometimes put a strain on the budget. Additionally, we financed the purchase of the commercial building with our local bank.

Running a business requires long hours. Operating out of my home meant I had to split my time between my own children and a houseful of other kids. I believe, however, that Nanny's Kids Inc. has contributed to the local economy, and the goodwill with the community has really added value to my business.

Starting and running a business is really hard work, and it's something that takes serious dedication, but it's worth every minute.

CHAPTER 9

THE
DEAL

The key issues covered in this chapter are:

- *Letter of Intent*
- *Due Diligence*
- *Representations and Warranties*
- *Negotiating from the Buyer's Seat*
- *Negotiating Guidelines*
- *The Closing Process*

There are several objectives to be accomplished during this process other than the goal of negotiating the best price possible. The terms of the deal, once negotiated, will have far-reaching consequences for the buyer and the seller. The terms of the deal can affect available cash reserves, tax rates, capital gains on investments, legal issues, and the profitability of the business over a number of years. But prior to the negotiations, there is a letter of intent, which is the basis for all future negotiations, so we would be remiss if we did not begin this chapter with a discussion of this document. Although it is a pre-contractual document that is sent prior to the onset of negotiations, it is, nonetheless, a very important element in the negotiation process.

THE LETTER OF INTENT

The letter of intent puts into writing what has up until this point been an exercise in oral negotiation between the buyer and seller. Even though you may be an experienced buyer or seller and you're working with an experienced intermediary, you should involve your legal counsel before proceeding. The lawyer you've retained should be involved in the writing of the letter of intent as a matter of course simply because this instrument will be the foundation upon which all future legal and binding discussions are based.

We're going to list the key elements of the letter of intent here, not necessarily in order of importance or even layout, but in the chronological order of occurrence:

1. The price of the business.

2. The form of purchase and what exactly is being purchased.

3. The structure of the purchase: cash, stock, non-compete agreements, earn-outs, and structured or seller-financed options.

4. Management contracts and/or agreements.

5. Closing costs and the specific responsibilities of the buyer and seller for due-diligence expense and title searches.

6. Representations and warranties.

7. Brokerage fees.

8. Timeline for closing and completion of sale.

9. Insurance.

10. Disposition of earnings prior to closing and any non-ordinary expenditures prior to closing.

11. Access to books, records, financials, customers, and employees prior to closing.

12. Disclosure of any non-financial agreements or obligations.

13. Stipulation of confidentiality.

14. Seller agreement to remove the business from the market for a customary period of 45 to 60 days.

Once the intermediary or maybe even the buyer makes the seller aware of the fact that a letter of intent is going to be forthcoming, there are certain pieces of data the buyer or buyers will need in order to draft the letter of intent:

1. Annual financial statements.

2. List of shareholders and key managers with all details pertinent to ownership, age, current position, years of service, salary, and any bonus or incentive plans.

3. List of all contractual obligations.

4. List of all major customers and the annual sales volume for each.

5. List of accounts receivable at signing.

6. Add-backs or earning adjustments that would probably not be incurred under new ownership.

7. Real estate, machinery, and equipment appraisals (if any).

8. Breakdown of inventory by stage of completion.

9. Amount and description of capital expenditures over the last five years and any estimate of future needs.

10. If stock purchase, copy of loan documents.

11. If stock purchase, listing of life insurance policies with named insured, face value, cash surrender value, and annual premium.

At this juncture, the letter of intent is ready to be delivered, and it is at this time that the earnest discussions begin. Usually, when the buyer and seller strike a deal, the sooner the buyer can secure the financing, complete the due diligence, and draft the purchase and sell agreement, the less chance both parties will have to change their minds. After the letter of intent is signed, an expedited closing can take place between 60 and 90 days assuming there are no major problems encountered that have not already been anticipated. It is a very difficult and time-consuming job to bring the deal to a successful close.

Make no mistake about the importance of the letter of intent and this particular stage in the buy/sell relationship. Almost 50 percent of all deals fail at the letter-of-intent stage. The fallout continues until you reach the negotiating table and begin to close the deal. Only 10 percent of all potential deals make it to closing.

Below is a checklist of the items you will see in a letter of intent. It is very important that you understand each element and that you are aware of your rights and responsibilities when executing this document.

One important point to remember during the furnishing of information to the buyer is that you as a seller have the right to receive financial information about the buyer in order to be assured that he or she can actually secure the funding necessary to complete the purchase.

Although the letter of intent is a non-binding agreement if so stated, you should devote careful attention to it not only because it is the precursor to the purchase agreement, but because it puts into writing the terms of a proposed transaction and gives the principals a feeling that they have reached an understanding. It also has a profound effect on the definitive documentation of the transaction.

Checklist of Items in a Letter of Intent

This is what you will see when you receive or submit a letter of intent:

1. Description of the buying organization, such as place of business and owners.

2. Statement of price, structure, contingencies, and exactly what is being purchased.

3. Description of any notes—their interest rates, terms, and amortization provisions and whether they're secured or unsecured, negotiable or non-negotiable. Will the buyer have the right to offset part of the note

if the seller does not meet certain conditions in the purchase and sell agreement?

4. Specification of management contracts—for whom, duration, and incentives.

5. Explanation of closing costs including intermediaries' fees spelling out who pays what.

6. A statement that representations and warranties will be a part of the purchase and sell agreement.

7. Description of profit-sharing arrangements.

8. A list of contingencies that have to be resolved in order for the transaction to be completed (environmental studies, title transfers).

9. Planned changes to be made such as management and continuity items. (Will the business be relocated?)

10. Estimated date of closing.

11. Transferability of insurance.

12. Reconciliation of debts or collections with shareholders.

13. Continuity of business until closing date.

14. Access to books and records.

15. Description of consulting and non-compete agreements.

16. The adherence to confidentiality by both parties and the understanding that the letter of intent is non-

binding and that the seller will take the company off the market for a specified period of time.

17. A consideration of whether the parent company (if there is one) should also sign the letter of intent and/or if the guarantors of the selling company's obligations (if there are any) should also sign the document.

18. Whether to create an escrow account to handle post-closing adjustments to the purchase price to reflect changes in inventory, final audited financials, or collections of accounts receivable to offset seller's contractual claims.

NEGOTIATIONS

After the letter of intent is drafted and delivered and signed by both parties, what is the next step? The due-diligence process on the part of the buyer begins, and the stage is set for the second round of negotiations. Let me guess: You didn't realize that negotiations had begun? They haven't formally; however, the letter of intent can only be drafted after serious talks and meetings between the buyer and seller have taken place, and its entire purpose is to state in writing the agreed-upon elements of the purchase agreement. It is the early stage of the negotiating process.

As the buyer begins the due-diligence process, the seller can begin to request financial information from the buyer to determine ability to fund the purchase, and both parties should make the following decisions: the negotiation strategies each party should use, the top and bottom acceptable prices, the key issues for each party, and anticipation of the other party's responses. Let's begin by identifying and explaining the different negotiation strategies that may be used. There are basically only three approaches to use:

1. **Take it or leave it.** This approach requires extreme discipline, or an extreme lack of interest. Perhaps you are making the best offer possible as the buyer and there is not another alternative. In this case, this approach would serve you well since you can't really negotiate.

2. **Split the difference.** During the negotiation, the buyer may make a low offer, and the seller may ask a high price. The split-the-difference approach can be used to meet in the middle. This technique can also be applied to other key issues, especially those to which a dollar value has been assigned.

3. **This for that.** This is a common strategy used when neither side can assign a dollar value to a particular issue but wish to reach some sort of compromise. If you will give this, I will give that. There are generally several key elements of the buy/sell agreement that have a non-monetary value. It is extremely helpful to be prepared to negotiate these terms without the use of the dollar.

Once the decision is made about strategy, the next move is toward pricing, key issues, and the anticipated responses.

High-End/Low-End Price Issue

By now, you are aware of the realistic valuation that has been placed on the business, whether buyer or seller, and you need to decide now rather than in the heat of the moment what you will or won't accept in relation to the final price for purchase or sell.

Frequently Negotiated Issues

Believe it or not, there are typical issues that are negotiated no matter what the business, industry, or market. The most frequently negotiated issues are:

- Price

- Deal structure

- Management/employee concerns

- Non-compete/contractual clauses

Anticipating Your Opponent's Responses

This is perhaps the most difficult aspect of preparing for the negotiating process. It is never easy to anticipate what the other party is going to do or how they are going to react. Your ability to quickly assess a response and act upon it can mean the difference between success and failure at the negotiating table.

DUE DILIGENCE

Due diligence as a part of the negotiation must be no less than perfect. Due diligence is performed on the non-financial, financial, and legal records of the business in order to verify that the information that has been furnished is accurate. Every aspect of your future and the business's future will depend on verification of information. Careful planning and expert advice will ensure successful due diligence. The information you will need to complete the due-diligence process is covered extensively in Chapter 4: The Evaluation; however, it is during this process of due diligence where you will take the information discussed in Chapter 4 and put together an agreement that includes all pertinent pieces of information that will either protect you or leave you exposed at the end of the negotiations. Both parties must be acutely aware of the importance of the due-diligence process. The three basic areas of due diligence are financial, legal, and business. If you've been reading this book straight through, you probably have a pretty good idea about the information examined during each part; if not, we're going to make sure you have a general understanding of each area and the information you need to review.

Financial due diligence refers to an intensive examination of the business books. Sales, cost of goods, and labor are only minor pieces of the puzzle. One method that often reveals discrepancies in accounting figures is the comparison of tax returns to actual financial statements; if there are huge differences in numbers there, you need to dig deeper. If everything checks out, move on to the accounts receivables, payables and inventory. Are there any dead accounts? Is there any obsolete inventory listed on the asset sheet? Look also at expenses; are there any major changes in the industry that would affect the expense associated with operating the business? Discrepancies can be used to negotiate a reduced selling price.

Legal due diligence investigates territorial information, status of contracts, any existing legal liabilities, any pending legal liabilities, contract services, and lease and equipment purchase conditions. In addition, you should also look at any legal repercussions, such as binding contracts with suppliers that lock the company into certain buying levels or price structures.

Business due diligence examines the products; the market; the surrounding economic conditions, if applicable; competitors; legislation that could affect the business; and any expected industry changes that could impact the profitability of the business.

You can never know too much about a business. It is here that you need general knowledge of the business arena you're entering and a network of associates that can give you inside information about any upcoming industry or market changes.

Deal structures are tremendously affected by your ability to negotiate; in fact, the deal structure is one of the prime targets of the negotiation process. What type of deal can we work out here? The buyer needs the seller to finance; the seller needs a way to avoid capital-gains tax. The art and skill of the negotiator will either create a win-win situation for both buyer and seller, or the parties involved may reach an impasse. It is typically during the detailed arrangements of the deal structure where you reach a make-or-break situation. Let's look at the most often-used deal structures once more, and look at them from the negotiator's perspective. This often makes or breaks the negotiations.

Seller-financed mortgages make up some 90 percent of all small business financing. Quite often, seller financing is a result of the negotiation process and can serve to assure potential sellers of some level of continued contact with a business and buyers of the necessary capital funding to close the deal. There are as many ways to use this option as there are buyers and sellers. The use of structured buyout deals, earn-out options, and seller retention of interest in the business are the most popular, but they are not the only method for completing the sale of a business. The reason seller-financed mortgages are so popular with small businesses is that all too often traditional lending institutions will not lend the necessary amount of capital to bridge the gap between the buyer's personal investment and the seller's asking price; goodwill is not as easily established and verified when dealing with small businesses, and many of the venture capitalists are simply not in the market for small, privately held businesses. The best alternative: seller financing.

Structured buyouts often include a promissory note to the seller to be paid at a later date, assuming the business remains operational and profitable. Although on the surface this seems a bit risky, if the seller has been upfront concerning non-financial business issues, and the buyer is well qualified to operate a small business, the likelihood of success and eventual payment of the promissory note are great. Other spin-offs on this particular arrangement include the seller's continued input on a contractual basis. As a seller, there is more assurance of success and eventual receipt of the final payout if you are still an active participant in the business, even in a smaller way. You are still available to help the new owner transition into the business and hopefully minimize mistakes that create losses, but you are not ultimately responsible for operations.

Earn-outs are a better deal for the buyer than for the seller, unless the buyer and seller have extreme confidence in each other and have a trusting relationship. Ultimately, the seller is at the buyer's mercy; the seller must depend on the buyer to accurately report earnings in order to assess the earn-out amount if it is based on percentages; if not, accuracy is simply necessary for a yes or no situation. Yes, we made money, so here is yours; or no, we didn't make money, so you don't get the earn-out pay.

The thing you must remember when structuring your deal is that the options are many, and the details are as varied as the individuals involved. Every deal is different; therefore, every deal structure is different. You, as a buyer or seller, have the opportunity to work out an arrangement that may only work for your unique situation; that's perfectly acceptable. Since very few buyouts actually involve a lending institution such as a bank, there is very little federal regulation to be concerned with, and this makes for a plethora of possibilities.

Representations and Warranties

Representations and warranties are traditionally included in the purchase and sell agreement that is normally provided at the onset of the serious buyer's offer. They are included during the closing information for a reason: the representations and warranties are one of the most highly scrutinized and negotiated topics during the closing process. For the purposes of this book, we're going to define exactly what a buyer or seller should seek in the representations and warranties made during the closing process; beyond that, each situation will present unique circumstances and unique representations and warranties. I would recommend, however, that you seek legal counsel when completing this piece of your closing process.

The representations and warranties are such an important part of the negotiations that should any of the representations and warranties prove untrue, the buyer is able to fully back out of the agreement without any repercussions, and in fact will have the option to sue the buyer for falsely representing the business. What are the most important and most-often-included representations and warranties?

The buyer should have a closing audit performed because it is imperative to verify the authenticity of all the terms, inventory, receivables, and payables. A post-closing adjustment is factored into the final purchase and sell agreement sometimes as an escrow account.

The buyer must be assured that the assets are being transferred with full assignability, especially such items as intellectual property, patents, property, etc. There should also be an assurance that all machinery and equipment are in good condition and working order.

It is absolutely critical to verify the seller's tax liability, especially if it is a stock purchase, since all corporate liabilities will transfer upon sale. Check for liens, delinquencies, and pending tax litigation.

Employment contracts and employee benefit programs must be fully disclosed as the new owner would not want to create a hostile atmosphere with employees by taking away agreed-upon incentives.

Many deals today are being cancelled due to environmental violations or liabilities. The expense associated with an environmental violation or ordered cleanup of contamination can be astronomical; a buyer would not want to be held responsible for an occurrence that happened prior to ownership that could potentially cause the business to fail.

Quite often, the buyer will inherit some of the risk for prior products, especially if the business is a manufacturing facility, but the buyer doesn't want to inherit pending litigation that will call for automatic monetary payout.

The seller must have any necessary authorization to sell the business from stockholders, directors, and/or third-party investors or banks.

To sum up this document, the seller will be expected to ensure to the buyer the following:

1. All liabilities are represented.

2. All contracts are disclosed.

3. All wages and taxes are current.

4. All insurance is current.

5. All bonus plans are disclosed.

TROUBLED COMPANIES AND SPECIAL CONSIDERATIONS

The special considerations that must be given to the company or business in management, financial, or operational trouble warrant some attention during the negotiations process. Quite often, all of the material discussed previously will be complete or nearing completion regardless of the state of the business's health. It is at this juncture in the process, the negotiations and the structuring of the deal, that the special considerations of a troubled company begin to be of importance. There are some key aspects that each side, buyer and seller, should consider in coming to the negotiating table with a troubled company on the line.

Leverage issues: re-capitalization, turnaround specialists,

structured buyouts, management concessions, cash flow, and time constraints all come into play in the sale of a troubled company. This brief section attempts to make the reader aware of the special opportunities as well as the pitfalls created when negotiating for a troubled business.

Re-capitalization refers to situations in which a troubled business leverages its debt-to-equity position in order to keep the company alive or operational. Suppose your employees wanted to buy out your ownership in the business; they could undergo a leveraged re-capitalization and effectively buy out your shares for ownership. This isn't seen too often in small business situations, but it does occasionally happen.

Other troubling situations can arise from poor management—a lack of focus, loss of key personnel, and other less-visible internal deficiencies. Often, these situations can be corrected by what is known as "turnaround specialists," and often these individuals will buy the business prior to turning it around, allowing the specialist to make wonderful profits from a successful turnaround.

The other great contributor to the sale of troubled companies will most often stem from a lack of adequate cash flow; in small businesses, especially those that are founder-operated, there is the potential for tremendous cash problems if the founder must retire or suddenly be incapacitated. The business does not usually keep a reserve of cash or other value since most of any of the accumulated wealth each year is paid out to family members; therefore, when a business like this has a slow year or a decline in sales, there isn't any cash reserve to help see it through.

These troubling situations are golden opportunities for the right buyer; any problems, no matter how small, are opportunities to re-negotiate price, buyout terms, deal terms, even financing options. We have included a somewhat extensive discussion here because these businesses are often the best market buys.

NEGOTIATING FROM THE BUYER'S SEAT

Negotiating from the buyer's seat, there are some key concepts you need to understand, exemplify, and carry with you to the negotiating table. These are listed here, and a brief discussion of each is given.

Style refers to the particular approach you will use in conducting the negotiations; should you allow the intermediary to take the floor, or should you make it a joint effort? Quite often, it works to your benefit to allow the intermediary to conduct most of the negotiations and for you step in only when concessions are absolutely necessary. The negotiations remain more controlled and less volatile when intermediaries are allowed to conduct the majority of the conversations.

Information refers to just that: obtain as much information as possible prior to the negotiation. You can never know too much about your opponent, and you should never underestimate their knowledge about you.

Leverage addresses any weaknesses that either party brings to the table. Know yours and your opponent's prior to beginning negotiations.

Brainstorming should occur between yourself and your advisory team prior to beginning negotiations; know your options, your opportunities, and your limitations before you begin.

Anticipate the actions of your opponent. Learn to trust your instincts during the flow of the negotiations; if you're prepared mentally and emotionally and are armed with all available knowledge, you'll find that you're able to readily adapt to a fluctuating situation and swing things in your favor.

Presentation of your case is an important consideration. Present a valid argument based on sound reasoning that validates how and why you arrived at your proposed price.

Controlling issues (price) is the climax of the entire process for the negotiators. If it is stated too quickly, you may fail to hold the other party's attention; if you wait too long, you may be forced to work with a ridiculously high and unreasonable number from your opponent. The best way to handle the price issue is to know when to address it and take control of the issue at that point.

Non-price issues (terms) — you may have heard the saying that the seller sets the price; the buyer sets the terms. In many situations, this is so. If you are truly involved and both parties seek a successful close, this just may be the case. If you're the buyer, you need to remember this.

Bluffing can be very valuable, but don't play this game unless you're disciplined enough to play and win and you have full knowledge of your limits.

Reaching the deal should come at the end of all these proceedings. If you're successful, you walk away with a compromise that is acceptable to both parties. It is now that you draft and execute a buy/sell agreement. This is generally done by the buying party as it gives better control over the document and the process (especially terms).

Negotiating Guidelines

Negotiating guidelines are discussed here, just as the rules of any game are explained prior to the onset of the game. Although negotiations are not generally a game, there are some similarities. You have an opponent, your objective is winning, and strategic knowledge will be required to win. What are the most obvious and necessary rules for negotiation?

- **Preparation.** Here we are referring to you, whichever party you may be. Be ready. Know your limits, what you can and cannot actually walk away from the table and live with. Price, terms, demands, and concessions will all be discussed at the negotiating table. Know your limits, your situation, and your resources.

- **Presentation.** You are no different from the lawyer arguing his or her case; make it good. Present a valid case for your decisions and conclusions; be able to back up your price, terms, and other non-price issues.

- **Demeanor.** The attitude you take to the negotiating table is crucial. Never underestimate the power of your attitude in affecting the other parties.

- **Options.** Know what your options really are prior to arriving. Know what you can concede, what terms you can affect, and how best to walk away successful.

- **Preserve the relationship.** Above all, behave in a manner that will preserve the relationship you have with the other party. If things are spiraling out of control, take a break; a few minutes or a few days are not that much to give in order to achieve a successful close.

- **Remedies.** What are remedies and what role do they play in the negotiations? Remedies are the options being offered by either party, but usually the seller, that provide for opting out of some condition of the buy/sell agreement should one party find the other has misrepresented some part of the information provided. Liabilities, sales issues, customer lists and contracts, liens, lawsuits, back taxes, and nondisclosure issues are all grounds for exercising the remedies available. What does this do to the negotiations? It is the conscience of the negotiators; each party is aware that there will be repercussions if all parties involved are not upfront and forthcoming with their representations and warranties.

THE CLOSING PROCESS

The end of all your hard work should not net results that are anything less than a tremendous success; but just because you've reached the closing phase of your buy or sell proposal doesn't mean your work is finished. In fact, some of your most arduous and demanding work is just about to begin. Due diligence, deal structuring, and representations and warranties require the attention to detail that many individuals simply do not have the knowledge or experience to properly execute. There are legal, financial, and business concerns that must be addressed in each of the three areas. If you haven't had the occasion to use your team of advisors, now is the perfect time.

A financial review should be conducted by an outside party; sometimes this is a requirement made during the negotiations, especially if there is seller financing; this guarantees that there will be periodic checks performed by an uninterested third party to ensure that the new owners aren't experiencing financially crippling problems.

Non-financial issues that were addressed during the negotiation process should be reviewed once more for clarification.

Employee, vendor, and customer input should begin in earnest at this juncture. It's time to get in there and really get to know what you've purchased, from the employees up.

There are four key elements to be concluded prior to closing:

1. Both parties have agreed to the price and terms and the seller has shown evidence that he or she has legal authority to sell the business.

2. Due diligence has been completed by the buyer, and the seller's representations and claims have been substantiated.

3. The financing is secured and the proper liens are in place so that the lender can release the funds for the acquisition financing.

4. Remedies are available to the buyer if the seller breaches the representations and warranties.

Once these elements are set in place, hopefully, you have closed negotiations in a satisfactory and successful way; you're now on your way to owning and operating a business.

Before we move to the final goal of ownership and transition, let's take a moment to review some of the finer points of buying and selling a business, and highlight some important aspects to remember:

1. The decision to sell is not irreversible; you can change your mind. It may have cost you to prepare to sell, but that is a small price for ultimate satisfaction.

2. Before you begin any process, decide who will be in charge. Who will negotiate, make final decisions, and be in charge of the general selling.

3. Pick your professional advisors and then listen to them. They are knowledgeable in their areas of expertise and you are not.

4. Communicate effectively with all members of your advisory team; utilize their knowledge and skills through effective and constant communication.

5. Negotiate non-compete and stay agreements between yourself, the prospective buyer, and your top employees.

6. Follow the buy/sell recommended procedures as laid out in this and other instructional books. This process will lead to success and does protect both parties if used correctly.

7. Set up plans and timelines in order to stay the course and stick with your plan.

8. Establish search criteria and know what you're looking for before you begin the process of looking for a buyer or seller.

9. Take the time necessary to perform the self-evaluation. You must know you before you can effectively lead other people.

10. Keep the deal structure as simple as possible. The more complex you make the deal, the harder it is to enforce.

11. Do your homework before you begin negotiations; choose your strategy once you are familiar with your opponent.

12. Perform the due diligence with the help of an attorney and an accountant at the very minimum.

13. Make sure you understand and are comfortable with the valuation methods discussed here and that you decide which method or combination to use.

14. If you're the seller, be prepared to negotiate terms; if you're the buyer, be prepared to negotiate the price.

15. Fully research the representations and warranties. Know the business you're proposing to buy.

16. Understand the reason the business is for sale.

17. Know your opponent.

18. Know the industry, the competition, and the target market.

19. Be flexible.

20. Use intermediaries and let them do their jobs.

During the closing process, you're actually taking the first steps into the transition phase, and this is the topic of the final chapter in this book. It's just as important to make a smooth transition as it is to complete negotiations successfully. Let's take a look now at your final destination: your transition to business owner.

CASE STUDY

WJV Trucking is a trucking operation that is independently owned and operated in the logging industry as a contract carrier. The business was started as the alternative option when a local manufacturing company moved overseas. The owner has a high school diploma, but jobs are scarce in the area, and trucking is the prevalent occupation for many of the local citizens.

Contact Information: W. Jason Vice
121 Vice Road
Kennedy, AL 35574

I started WJV Trucking because I had to have an income, and I could drive a truck. The demand for drivers and trucks is always a constant in this area. The southeast is one of the biggest contributors of lumber to the construction industry. My knowledge of driving a truck, good work ethic, and commitment to my business have all contributed to my success. Owning my own business has afforded me the ability to make my own decisions and to work for myself. It's also increased my earning ability.

Alternately, the hours are sometimes long, and contract hauling is very frustrating at times. The capital needed to start the business was a huge challenge because trucks are very expensive. I borrowed the money needed to purchase the startup equipment, and my accountant helped me establish a value, by using a combination of EBIT and asset-based valuation, on the type of business I had wanted to start. My accountant and lawyer handled all the legal and tax issues involved with starting WJV Trucking.

Today, WJV Trucking has grown and contributes to the economic value of the community.

I recommend small business ownership if you're sure you want to own your own business; it's been a great opportunity for me.

CASE STUDY

NRV Investment Properties is an individually owned-and-operated real estate enterprise that was formed as a way to develop residual income and investment opportunity in anticipation of building a retirement asset.

Contact Information: Michelle Busch
7918 Sonny Ridge
San Antonio, TX 78244

I started NRV Investment Properties to develop an asset for retirement income. Real estate was the obvious choice because it's one of the best ways to establish residual income. Thus far, it has helped to grow my net worth and to provide an excellent lucrative asset. I've also learned so much about investing, real estate, and how to build wealth.

Owning a business is very time consuming and can often be frustrating when you're looking for rental investment property and developing a responsible renter base. In fact, it can be costly to make mistakes with renters.

However, with the help of a real estate agent, I was able to make the best decisions for my business, and I obtained financing from a local lending institution. To handle the legal issues involved with buying a business, I hired lawyers and accountants. It was necessary for us to go through due diligence.

Today, because of commitment and dedication to the development of my retirement income, NRV Investment Properties has become a valuable asset, contributing to the economic value of the community.

I would absolutely recommend small business ownership to others. It's been a long learning process, but I've learned so much and have been able to grow my assets and retirement income.

CHAPTER 10

THE TRANSITION

The key issues covered in this chapter are:

- *You as the Buyer or Seller*
- *Post-Closing Evaluations*
- *Learning to Manage from a Different Perspective*
- *Maintaining Key Relationships*

YOU AS THE BUYER OR SELLER

As you step into the role you have now assumed as an owner, or by stepping out of the role you've been playing as business owner, you have made a tremendous change in your life. Your ability to successfully implement this change lies in your knowledge of yourself, your management skills, and your flexibility and adaptability.

Let's take a look at the seller's position first: You are now simply a member of the management, hired as a consultant to advise the new owner. You must effect a change in yourself and in your former employees who will still have a tendency to turn to you for their directives, not the new owner. Maintaining an excellent working relationship with the new owner and your former employees will take tremendous diplomacy on your part and a bit of luck. Your best option for dealing with this change is to conduct a joint meeting of former and new owners and employees. You need to announce the new situation to your former employees and effect the change of attitude and environment in one action. You should also include what's known as a post-closing evaluation as part of your list of things to do. From either side of the agreement, making notations and evaluations at this point will be a tremendous asset later.

POST-CLOSING EVALUATIONS

After you have completed the sale, from either position, you should take a day or two to look back, reflect, make notes, and compile a journal of sorts. Many individuals start a journal at the beginning of this process and therefore simply need to make closing entries. If you didn't begin a journal at the onset, take some time now to put together the information you want to retain for future reference. Now that you've come through the fire, so to speak, make notes that will allow you to retain what you've learned, and to continue to learn from it. Listed below are a few items you'll want to include in this post-closing evaluation, and there are probably areas that are unique to your situation. Add them as well.

Communication: Did you communicate well with the parties involved in the process: your intermediary, your financier, your accountant? Was the necessary level of confidentiality maintained by all parties involved? Did you effectively communicate your wants and needs during the negotiation process?

Preparation: How well did you prepare for the buy/sell process? Did you compile comprehensive information that was useful to your advisory team? to the other party? to you? Did you prepare your business or your search criteria well? What about the selling memorandum? Was it accurately prepared? The letter of intent? All these elements came together to make the deal a success; were you pleased with the end result?

Pricing: Did you carefully put together an accurate picture of your business and its value? Did you assemble comparables? Did you need comparables? Did you accurately value your intangibles?

Negotiating: Were you satisfied with your efforts to choose the most beneficial strategy? Did your negotiations net you what you expected? Were you and your intermediary (if you had one) prepared when you reached the negotiation stage?

Closing: Was the closing of the deal reached to your satisfaction? Could you have done more to prepare and articulate to your negotiating team what you wanted and expected? Did you or your attorney structure the deal in order to provide future protection from incorrectly reported representations and warranties?

LEARNING TO MANAGE FROM A DIFFERENT PERSPECTIVE

From the new buyer's position, the change that has just taken place will effect a tremendous change in the lives of the buyer and the buyer's family. Now he must take the reins and develop the business in his or her chosen direction. If you have never taken any form of management training, now is the time. I would suggest that you take the time to enroll in a course prior to the completion of the buy/sell agreement. Your ability to effectively handle your new employees and provide the leadership they need will have a tremendous impact on your business for the next several months.

However, there are a few items that must be addressed that are not directly related to the business but can have long-lasting effects for the business. First, take a moment to acknowledge your family—your spouse or your spouse and children. The days of bringing about the sale are often just as stressful for family members as they are for the buyer or seller. Take a moment to thank them.

Second, make sure you let the individuals that were involved in the business aspects of bringing the sale to a close know how much you appreciate their help also. After all, you may want or need their help in the future; and business associates, consultants, or professional appraisers appreciate those who appreciate them.

Third, get to know your new employees, from the least important to the most important. They need to know that the new owner is interested in their work and his or her new business.

Fourth, take some time during the first month to meet any major vendors, suppliers, customers, or distributors. Making personal contact with these individuals puts a face to the name and a personal touch to the relationship.

And last, but not least, make time during the first few weeks to note the feedback you receive from the employees, customers, vendors, suppliers, and any other personnel directly associated with the business. Often, it is through constructive criticism or feedback that previously untapped markets and revenue are discovered.

Once you've made a point of being seen and of seeing the personnel with whom you will interface as a business owner, get to know your new business. Take several days to observe. Perform what's known as a SWOT (strengths, weaknesses, opportunities, and threats) analysis of the business, from the insider's viewpoint. You may or may not have had a professional business appraiser perform this type of analysis during the due diligence, but that was from a potential buyer's viewpoint. Now you need an analysis from the owner's viewpoint.

The SWOT analysis will make you aware of internal and external elements that affect the business and, in turn, can and do affect the bottom line. Although many new managers do not take advantage of the analytical tools and resources that are available, it is in your best interest to perform an initial assessment. You can better determine short-range goals and directions if you are well informed about your starting position.

During the course of the analysis, make a note of any problems observed, process improvements that could be implemented or any issues that merit your attention, but don't change anything. Leave the current policies and procedures in place until you have performed a thorough analysis of the existing operations. Sometimes we don't fully understand all the repercussions that a change to a particular procedure or process can have on other areas.

MAINTAINING KEY RELATIONSHIPS

Employees and management are as great a concern for the new business owner as the customers and vendors also acquired during the transaction. The new business owner will need to rely heavily on the knowledge and expertise of the existing work force for several months before he or she has a firm grasp on much of the day-to-day operations. This is something many first-time business owners fail to understand. You should make it a point shortly after taking control to meet with all the employees, managers, and any contract personnel to answer questions they may have and to communicate your intentions for the business. Employees today are quite fearful of ownership changes and often anticipate the worst; it is up to you to alleviate any fears they may have and to give them direction under the new leadership. In dealing with general employees, if possible, take the time to interview each one either individually or in small groups. Provide a broad overview of your intentions, ask for their input, and listen when feedback is given. Quite often, you can save yourself mistakes by simply listening to your new employees. As you get to know your employees, make it a point to casually observe work flow and job responsibilities and make a note of any possible improvements. Often, with small businesses, there is no clear communication of job responsibilities, and employees tend to operate in a somewhat freelance mode. Review your management team and meet with the managers individually to discuss their current responsibilities, to obtain feedback about their job responsibilities, and to understand their supervisory responsibilities. You will very likely find there has been no formal management training and that the supervisory skills do not provide adequate direction for the employees immediately under their supervision.

Management and key-personnel retention at the early stages can be quite crucial. Since you're new to the process, you're going to need to rely on their expertise to help you get started. Meet with these people immediately. Make them aware of your purposes and intentions and any major changes. Be sure to let them know you appreciate their presence.

Vendors and customers acquired during the buy/sell transaction are generally quite receptive to new owners provided there are no pre-existing issues. You should not neglect this area as you absorb information about your new company; although not always present, they are the reason you will stay in business. Many new owners hold open houses or receptions in an attempt to further solidify business relationships. Sometimes specials are offered as promotional get-acquainted offers that will provide some incentive for customers to come and meet the new owners.

Other professionals associated with the business will probably want to meet you, such as bankers, accountants, lawyers, etc. These people can also be crucial to the immediate success of the business and developing positive relationships here can only serve to benefit you later.

Name retention is generally done for one of two purposes: It was a negotiated part of the buy/sell agreement, or the new owner simply anticipates that keeping the former owner's name will increase the likelihood that the new business will succeed. Many times when ownership changes, the name of a small business will also change, and this can sometimes work against the new owners. Name association and recognition are valuable in retaining customers and employees and developing relationships with vendors. If you change an already well-established, successful business name, you lose all that goes with it. Even if you make changes to the business processes, the methods for conducting sales, and the employee policies, for those on the outside looking in, these changes aren't that noticeable, but the name continues to be an asset.

ABOVE ALL, KEEP LEARNING

Lastly, as an owner, you are the ultimate manager and supervisor. Bear in mind that the people under your supervision are only as good as their leader's direction. Remember that once you are involved in a business, it's much easier to see opportunities as they open up. And as long as you keep your mind open to all possibilities, you will be able to seize the moment.

As for yourself and your employees, encourage continuing education; you can never learn too much regardless of your position within a company. Learning opportunities for managers can later turn into teaching opportunities. If effectively led, anyone can learn the basics of good workmanship and effective leadership.

CASE STUDY

PJ's BBQ and Catering, Inc. is a locally owned-and-operated barbeque restaurant and catering business. The owner utilizes family members for most of her labor needs, and provides a warm and friendly personality for drawing customers and increasing sales. She also has some of the best barbeque in town!

Contact Information: Donna E. Blakney
617 18th Ave. N.
Columbus, MS 39701

I began PJ's BBQ and Catering, Inc. as a way to make a living. A restaurant and catering business was ideal because of my experience, work ethic, commitment, and knowledge of the local economy. I went into business with a friend, out of necessity, bought the business, and here I am.

The satisfaction of operating a successful business in my community has been the greatest advantage so far. In addition, my business has provided me with an excellent income and a tremendous capital investment.

The hard work, the amount of time that's needed to operate a restaurant, and the endless responsibility are challenges of owning a small business.

Finding the startup capital was also a challenge. When I found the business I wanted, I approached my partner. We sought outside financing, and in the restaurant business, it's almost impossible to get funding without additional real estate for collateral. We also sought seller-financing options.

When I purchased the business, my accountant used a combination of the methods to place a value on the business. My account and my lawyer handled the legal and tax issues of starting a business. We did perform due diligence prior to the purchase.

PJ's BBQ and Catering Inc. has grown, in part, through goodwill, and we've certainly contributed to the economic value of the community.

I would definitely recommend small business ownerships, but first make sure you fully understand the business, the area, the market you're depending upon for sales, and the local labor/employment base. Take a long look at the expense, income, and fixed costs. Then, if you're still sure you want to be in business, go for it!

CLASSIFIED CASE STUDIES
directly from the experts

CASE STUDY

Jan's Bakery provides a combination coffee shop and bakery in one location. As owner/operator, Jan likes to participate and interact with her patrons, as well as bake for them. This business was born of a need for additional income and a love of baking.

Contact Information: Jan Barnes
253 7th St. NW
Vernon, AL 35592

Jan's Bakery started as a way to supplement our family income. I had experience with baking, and thoroughly enjoy baking for my customers. I have a special-needs child that requires me to be at home, and this was the best way to bring in some extra money.

Having my own business has allowed me to continue to enjoy the extras of life. It keeps me active and allows me time to enjoy my children. The extra income provided from the business has been a necessity for me, not an option. The startup capital put tremendous restraints on my cash flow. All of my tax issues, however, are handled by my accountant.

Starting a business also takes long hours, and the business is always a responsibility. However, my love of baking and of people and my commitment have greatly contributed to my success. I know my customers truly enjoy their visits. Customer loyalty and word-of-mouth has helped me to grow at an astonishing rate.

I recommend small business ownerships; it's been a source of enjoyment and financial benefit for me.

CHAPTER 11

THE
REALITY

I n this final chapter, I'm going to tell you a few things about the realities of business entrepreneurship that you don't learn in a book—the things that you're going to experience and live if you have the opportunity to sit in the driver's seat. The entrepreneurial position isn't for everyone. As I stated in the beginning, it takes a special individual to be an entrepreneur.

There are no key issues covered in this final chapter. Here you will find some of the tools and pearls of wisdom that have pulled me through some really tough times when the outcome wasn't clear, times when my belief in my ability wasn't as firm as it is now, and times when failure seemed close at my heels

HOUSTON, WE HAVE A PROBLEM...

Entrepreneurship is not a free ticket past GO; it is a rollercoaster ride on a journey that will take you higher than you've ever been, and lower than you thought possible. Even so, I still say it's the best seat in the house.

During the early days of business ownership, you are going to need some pearls of wisdom to provide the moral boost that gets you from one endless day to another. There were passages I found that seemed to help tremendously and gave me guidance through some of the turbulence of the rollercoaster ride. I'm inclined at the end of this journey to share some of those passages with you in the hopes that you, too, will find inspiration, humor, and guidance.

Inspiration

The dictionary defines inspiration as "something such as a sudden creative act or idea that is inspired." That is exactly what you will need to feel about your leap into business ownership. You will need to draw on something greater than your average, ordinary, everyday feelings in order to keep pushing yourself and those around you. Inspiration can come to us in many different ways, forms, and ideas. What we gain from those moments of insight and bursts is that we have a higher purpose. We are the evolutionary exception to every other life form on this planet. We can choose. We can excel. We can overcome. If you never realize any other concept from this book, realize that there is a touch of the entrepreneurial spirit in us all. We may not choose to act on those urges, but we all have some level of the risk-taker within us. I've been blessed with the love of reading; and over the course of my life, I've run across many inspirational readings and verses. There are some verses I've found that help more than others, and I kept those around me as constant reminders of a higher purpose. I'm going to include a few here in the hopes that you will also find inspiration and strength.

How to really live life…

Dream Big. Why not? It makes life fun. Besides, if you don't have dreams, how are you going to have a dream come true?

Make mistakes. Then try to learn from them. If you never make mistakes, you're probably not trying anything new. Talk about boring!

Keep your mind open. That's how to catch the best ideas.

Extend yourself to others, especially those who are different from you. It makes life worthwhile, not to mention more interesting.

Delight in the natural world. Go outside and look at a tree every day. Or the sky. Learn to love the ordinary. It's the little things that get you by.

Develop deep inner resources. Be your own best company.

Have a happy life, one day at a time.

Then there is this old Irish proverb I discovered at the age of 12. I have kept these words close to my heart as a sort of life's creed.

Take time to work —
It is the price of success.
Take time to think —
It is the source of power.
Take time to play —
It is the secret of perpetual youth.
Take time to read —
It is the foundation of wisdom.
Take time to be friendly —
It is the road to happiness.
Take time to dream —
It is hitching your wagon to a star.

Take time to love and to be loved —
It is the privilege of the gods.

Take time to look around —
The day is too short to be selfish.
Take time to laugh —
It is the music of the soul.

Finally, be daring, bold and unafraid.
Go where no one has gone before.
Dance as if no one were watching,
Sing as if no one were listening,
And live every day as if it were your last.

Humor

What can we say about humor? Did you know that if you can find humor in your daily life, you will live longer? If you have the ability to perceive, enjoy, or express humor, you will get more out of life and certainly provide those who are a part of your life with a better daily quality of life. Why is this mentioned here? Because when you step into the shoes of the entrepreneur, the business owner, and the effective leader, it can become so easy to lose sight of anything humorous or fun. Everything that you're confronted with on a daily basis is of a serious nature, and if you don't take the time to find the humor in a situation, you lose sight of the reason you took on this project initially: to fulfill dreams, enrich your life, and bring about a change in the big picture.

Would you like to hear some interesting statistics? Read on for some facts about humor.

- Laughter induces more social behavior in people; in

other words they meet and enjoy each other's company more if there is laughter involved.

- Generally, we do not laugh unless we are with another person.

- Laughter is universal. It is one of the few human behaviors that crosses all lines of distinction and is recognized no matter your culture.

- Our brains are hardwired for laughter; it is an unconscious action.

- Humor and laughter brighten the work environment; it is an inducement to come to work if you're going to enjoy your time there.

Making people feel good about themselves is an attribute that not everyone is intuitively blessed with; however, you can develop this ability, and as you increase the esteem of others, you will see that your satisfaction with life also increases. I think this is where the old adage *It is better to give than to receive* comes from. What you give to others comes back to you many times over. This is also true of humor, praise, and goodwill.

What do these statistics say to you, the entrepreneur? If you want to keep employees, attract new customers, and/or keep already established business, make sure you include humor and good nature in your dealings with them all. There are times when humor may not be appropriate, but unless the situation dictates a serious demeanor, incorporate as much humor and sunshine as possible in it; you will likely be around longer and you will definitely have a greater circle of friends, employees, and business associates if you make them feel good.

Guidance

You must remember above all else that your purpose as a business owner is to lead the business toward success. If you neglect this responsibility, your business will fail. As with almost every business in existence today, you will have employees. You also have a responsibility to those individuals. They depend upon you and the success of your business to provide them with jobs, which in turn provide them with a steady income; your business and your employees are only as good as the leadership and guidance they receive. You won't learn how to be effective and be an excellent leader in a book. This comes from real-life application and a deep concern and care for the business and the employees who work in that business. I've found some excellent pearls of wisdom in this area also. It is a continual work in progress to be a good leader and to effect the motivation and guidance that a business and employees will need.

The Shipbuilder

Proverbs 11:14

"Where there is no leadership, the people fall…."

The Five Principles of Leadership

1. Make them feel appreciated.

2. See their potential, not their flaws.

3. Love them first.

4. Lead with authority, not power.

5. Make them feel they are a part of something special.

How Do You Really Succeed?

1. Create a plan.

2. Set deadlines to accomplish what you plan.

3. Do not waste your time.

4. If you have any contact with negativity, shut it out.

5. Stop listening to someone unless they're doing better than you.

6. Have fun.

7. Have a good attitude.

8. Take care of your health.

9. Stop thinking job.

10. Do for others.

Timing is of the essence no matter what you're undertaking; a clear understanding of the urgency of a situation or the fact that as time passes so does the opportunity is the basis for an understanding of timing. When you're in business, and you own the business, you won't receive a directive from higher up that an idea or process must be implemented. You are the higher up. You must know your customers, your industry, and your business capability well enough to know when opportunity presents itself and prepare to act upon the opportunity; in other words, seize the moment.

Having vision is not like "having a vision" (although you do sometimes). Having vision means that you can look ahead and see that changes are needed or that changes are coming and prepare your business to act upon that information. Visionaries are individuals who see what exists and then can see where something (people, industries, trends, etc.) are going. You must learn to develop this ability within yourself if you're going to be able to capitalize on opportunities before they come and go.

Taking action is absolutely necessary or the two previous qualities are of no value. If you understand the timing of a concept, have the vision to see it in use, but take no action to accomplish it, you have done nothing. Many would-be success stories never happen because no one acts on an idea. Ideas must take form, must come into existence through the human vehicle. In other words, once you have an idea, for it to come to fruition you must take some action; you must learn to push forward and be the initiator.

CASE STUDY

South Charter Enterprises is an owner-operated business that provides chartered boating excursions to tourists in the waters off the Gulf of Mexico. The business has been in existence for 11 years. To date, the owner has more work than he can handle. The question of additional boats has been a frequent one.

Contact Information: Wishes To Remain Anonymous

I started South Charter Enterprises to help offset the cost of a sports fishing vessel. Additionally, I have the boating skills, good work ethic, and dedication needed for a business to succeed. Small business ownership also helps offset the overhead, and it provides a way to meet new and interesting people, some of whom have been beneficial business contacts. Financially, the benefits have been increased income, tax deductions, and network opportunities.

The downside is the lack of weekend time off, which detracts from the time I have with my family. Furthermore, this type of business is seasonal, and its success is hinged on supply and demand. Licensing and charter expenses involved in this type of business are also substantial.

When I started, I had a lawyer handle the legal aspects of starting the business. There are many legal issues involved in licensing and operating a tourist/chartering vessel. I don't necessarily think my business has contributed the economic value of the community because this is a real tourist environment, and my business is not that large. However, goodwill has added value to the business.

I would recommend small business ownership, depending on the type of business. Regardless, it's essential to do extensive research first.

CASE STUDY

Scotty's Paints is an owner-operated business that provides automotive painting services to the general public. The business was formed as a means to make extra money on weekends and during vacations. It turned into a full-time venture after only four years as a sideline business.

> *Contact Information:* *Scotty Lawrence*
> *P.O. Box 179*
> *Vernon, AL 35592*

Scotty's Paints was born of a need for additional income for my family. Fortunately, I had the basic knowledge and skills because of some prior part-time apprentice work. I also had a strong knowledge of the equipment and how this type of business should be run. Of the many benefits of owning my own business are the extra income, growing the business, and the status that comes with business ownership.

Maintaining equipment can be costly, and I have purchased used painting equipment, which I financed through the seller. However, I have an accountant who takes care of the tax and other financial issues.

I recommended small business ownership. But first, research the business and everything involved with owning a business because there is always more than meets the eye.

CONCLUSION

C

This book is meant to provide the beginning entrepreneur with a basic outline of the steps involved in buying or selling small businesses; it does not by any means constitute an account of the actual journey that an individual will make during the self-discovery of buying, owning, and/ or selling a small business. It is one of the most rewarding opportunities for self-growth and discovery that exists today for the individual willing to commit.

The best that I can leave you with is some of the most beneficial advice I've ever been given: *You can't sell from an empty wagon, and you can't sell if the doors are closed!*

GLOSSARY

Add-backs: Extraordinary one-time expenses, such as the cost of moving. Add-backs are subject to acute scrutiny by the buyer because business travel and business entertaining are usually a regular cost of doing business.

Allocation of purchase price: In an asset sale, the purchase price must be allocated to certain assets; the balance is goodwill.

Angels: An individual high-risk investor who likes to make investments in promising acquisitions. Angels often have valuable business experience and can be helpful as members of the board of directors.

Asset-based lenders: Commercial lenders who are willing to take on more risk than commercial banks lending against accounts receivable and inventory and being subordinate to commercial banks.

Asset sale: Purchase of certain assets and/or liabilities leaving the seller the remainder as well as the corporate entity.

Audit: Examination of the financial records and accounting books in order to verify their accuracy.

Basket: A dollar amount set forth by the seller in the indemnification provision for any losses suffered by the buyer.

Book value: Also known as net worth, the figure derived by deducting all the liabilities from the entire asset.

Bottom fishing: When a buyer will only pay a very low price for a business.

Bridge-loans: A temporary loan to cover the financing shortfall of the acquisition until permanent funding is available.

C corporation: One of two types of corporation (the other is the S corporation). Taxes are paid once at the corporate level and again when the earnings are distributed to the shareholders. It allows various classes of stock: corporate shareholders as well as alien shareholders.

Cap-X: The acronym for capital expenditures that are necessary within the next year.

Capitalization: Companies have ownership capital that includes stock and paid-in surplus plus borrowed capital that includes bank debt and bonds. The combined forms of capital, ownership, and borrowed funds are a company's capitalization.

Capitalization rate: The conversion of income into value as part of the valuation process by the application of a capitalization factor (any multiplier or divisor used to convert income to value).

Cash cow: A business that has a steady cash flow in which earnings have remained nearly the same for the past five years but which has shown little growth.

Cash flow: The amount of

money left over after the cost of goods sold and general, selling, and administrative expenses but before interest, depreciation, taxes, and amortization.

Collateral: Property pledged by a borrower to protect the interests of the lender. Bank loans are often collateralized or secured by the company's accounts receivable, inventory, or equipment.

Confidentiality: The entrustment of proprietary information from one party to another for that party's exclusive use so as not to impart the obtained knowledge to others.

Contingent: Dependent on or conditioned by something else. The price established for the business varies in relation to some future event.

Contingent payments: Future financial obligations are dependent on contractual events that take place.

Covenants: A binding agreement between buyer and seller that restricts each party from taking certain actions particularly during the letter-of-intent period and closing.

Deal flow: A stream of potential business acquisitions moving across your desk in a quantity that allows you to select the few that meet your criteria.

Depreciation: The amount that tangible assets decrease over the normal life cycle as designated by the parameters of the IRS.

Discounted cash flow: A valuation technique that assigns a value in today's dollar to the cash flows that are expected to occur in the future.

Due diligence: The investigation of the other

party's business practices in an attempt to uncover previously unknown information.

Earn-outs: A part of the purchase price that is dependent on a future performance variable such as profits or sales.

EBIT: The acronym for earnings before interest and taxes.

EBITDA: The acronym for earnings before interest, taxes, depreciation, and amortization, also known as cash flow.

EBITDA-CAP-X: EBITDA minus capital expenditures. A more realistic assessment of earnings than EBITDA.

Encumbrances: A lien against certain property that encumbers the company's assets and that could ultimately hold up or prevent the closing.

Enterprise value: Market value of equity plus interest-bearing debt.

Entrepreneur: Taken from the German word "unternehmer," referring to a person who owns and runs his own business.

Escrow: Money delivered to a third party that is held in deposit until the grantee fulfills certain conditions.

Fair market value: What assets would most likely sell for in the open market; this is often determined by a professional appraiser.

Finder's fee: A commission for merely identifying and introducing a buyer to the seller; does not include other services such as valuing, structuring, and negotiating.

Floor price: The lowest preconceived price that a seller will accept.

Free cash flow: Operating income plus depreciation and amortization (non-cash charges) but subtracts capital expenditures and dividends (that use cash). Free cash flow, in essence, is the amount of cash left over after a year of business as usual.

GAAP: The acronym for generally accepted accounting principles; the American Institute of CPA's standards of accounting.

Goodwill: An intangible asset of a business that relates to a favorable relationship with customers and excess earning power.

Holdback provision: As written into the purchase and sell agreement if a buyer winds up having to pay a debt the seller did not disclose, the amount paid from that which was held back at closing in an escrow account.

I-banker: The abbreviation of investment banker; also known as a merger and acquisition intermediary and for smaller transactions known as a business broker.

Indemnification: Exemption for the buyer from incurred penalties after the closing from incomplete representations and warranties of the seller.

Intangibles: An asset that is not physical such as licenses, franchises, trademarks, customer lists, unpatented technology, etc.

Intermediary: An agent who is a merger-and-acquisition consultant to the buyer or seller and who is expected to facilitate the transaction.

Investment banker: An intermediary who often provides additional services such as bridge loans or underwritings.

Letter of intent: A preliminary offer to purchase a business, usually non-binding, which, if accepted by the seller, leads to the drafting of a purchase and sell agreement.

Leverage buyout: A transaction in which a company's capital stock or its assets are purchased with borrowed money causing the company's new capital structure to be primarily debt.

Lien: A charge or hold on assets usually by a creditor until the indebtedness is satisfied.

M & A: An initialism for mergers and acquisitions.

Market cap: Abbreviations for market capitalization that applies to the company's worth in the stock market by multiplying the total number of shares outstanding by the current price of the stock.

Middle market: Companies with sales between $2 million and $100 million.

Multiples: An abbreviated terminology for capitalization rates.

Net present value: Money paid out in the future discounted at the opportunity cost of capital for a similar risk over the specified period of time.

Net worth: See Book Value

Networking: Maintaining contacts with a variety of people connected with buying and selling businesses.

Niche: Uniqueness in the marketplace in which the company has a product or service, which has a competitive advantage because there are few competitors.

Off balance sheet items: Unrecorded obligations such

as repurchase agreements, pending lawsuits, and unfunded pensions.

OEM: Original equipment manufacturers produce products that are sold to other companies that in turn make products for consumer purchases.

Perquisites (perks): A profit incidental to a regular salary such as the use of a company automobile, country club membership, or entertainment allowance.

Representations and warranties: Indemnifications and covenants written into the purchase and sell agreement that provide factual information that is important to protect the buyer from future occurrences.

ROI (ROE): Return on investment and return on equity must be greater than the cost of capital in order to create shareholder value.

S corporation: Limited to 25 or fewer shareholders; this business structure limits each shareholder's liability (like a corporation), but profits and losses are reported by shareholders (like a partnership).

Seller financing: The seller extends his or her own notes to the buyer in lieu of all cash at closing or other debt financing, such as bank loans.

Senior debt: The most secure bank debt and the first in line with primary collateral. Often senior debt is a short-term revolving loan that is paid down completely within a year.

Stock sale: Purchase of the company's shares of stock incorporates the assumption of all the assets and all the debt both tangible and intangible.

Working capital: The balance between current assets and current liabilities represents the fund available to grow the business in the short-term.

CONFIDENTIALITY AGREEMENT

It's customary for the owner or CEO of the selling business to require the proposed buyer to sign a confidentiality statement or agreement. This is a general, non-specific format.

In connection with our interest in purchasing the assets and/ or stock of _____ (the Company), we have requested that we be permitted to examine the financial and other business records of the Company. We understand and agree that the information contained in these records is of a confidential nature and that it will be used by us solely for the purpose of making an offer for the assets and/or stock of the Company. We will not disclose, nor will our agents, servants, employees, or attorneys disclose any of the information contained in these financial and other business records, including the identity of the company, to any other person except to such investors, bankers, attorneys, or other persons necessary to consummate the sale to the undersigned.

Signed: _____
(Print)

Date:_____

_____
(Signature)

LETTER OF INTENT

_____ proposes to purchase all the
assets of _____ of _____,
_____ including goodwill, customer list, and all other
intangible and balance-sheet assets to be substantially the same
as those set forth on the balance sheet of _____
as of _____, Exhibit A. The name of the
business is transferred as an intangible asset.

1. Purchase Price. The purchase price for the assets will be
   $_____ payable in cash at closing.

2. Non-Compete Agreement. The principals of _____
   _____ agree not to compete, directly or indirectly,
   with the business of _____ as it pertains to
   _____ in any _____ market for a
   period of __ years, within a _____ radius.

3. Lease of Building. It is agreed that _____
   will use best efforts to transfer the lease to _____
   at current or market rental as permitted by the lease.

4. General and Specific Liabilities. _____
   will assume the liabilities as shown on the balance
   sheet dated _____, but will not assume any other

liabilities, past, present, or future.

5. Audit. _____ will cause to be conducted by _____ auditors at _____ expense as of a date to be selected.

6. Expenses. Each party to the Letter of Intent will pay their own expenses, including legal fees, up to the time of the closing. Any fees incurred during the process of due diligence shall be at the expense of the party requesting the information.

7. Letter of Intent. This Letter of Intent is nonbinding and may not be construed as an agreement on the part of any party. In the event that the parties are unable to agree on a mutually satisfactory definitive agreement providing for the transactions contemplated by this Letter of Intent, none of the parties shall be liable to any other party or to any other person. The conclusion of any definitive agreement will be subject to the following:

   a. Approval of all matters relating thereto by counsel for _____ and _____;

   b. Review of all business, legal, and auditing matters related to _____, the results of which are acceptable to _____.

   c. Approval of all matters related there by the proprietors, partners, or stockholders of

   _____.

   d. Completion of such financing as _____ may require to effect a closing.

e. Preparation and completion of all closing documents.

f. The closing date to take place in or within 90 days of the execution of the agreement.

g. Continuing of obligations. Until termination of the Letter of Intent, _____shall not, or any representatives, partners, or affiliated individuals, directly or indirectly, without prior written consent of _____ entertain negotiations with or make disclosures to any entity, group, partnership, proprietor, or individual in connection with any possible proposal regarding any merger, partnership, or sale of capital stock of _____, or of all or a substantial portion of the assets of _____, or any similar transaction.

h. Confidentiality. Both _____ and _____ agree to maintain complete confidentiality of all confidential material each company exchanges with the other as outlined in separate confidentiality agreements.

By: _____

Title: _____

Date: _____

By: _____

Title: _____

Date: _____

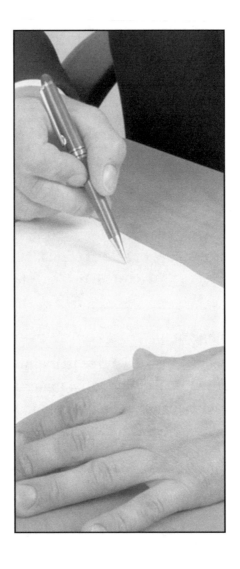

PROPOSAL LETTER

If a buyer expresses interest in your company after receiving the offering memorandum, you, as the seller, should request an indication of value in the form of a proposal letter such as the sample below.

It is not unusual to request such a letter prior to a visit to the company; you can waste a lot of time dealing with individuals not really interested in truly purchasing a valued business. If you do not have a planned and thorough offering memorandum, it is usual and customary to let the buyer visit with the seller and see the facilities.

Dear John Doe:

The following is a proposal to acquire the assets of Company B, Inc. (the "Company"). This letter is an outline of a proposed transaction and is not meant to be binding on any party at this time and is subject to the signing of a mutually acceptable, definitive Purchase and Sell Agreement. In addition, this offer is subject to the requisite due-diligence effort normally associated with a transaction of this magnitude. With the aforementioned kept in mind, our offer is as follows:

Transaction
A new corporation ("Company C") will be formed by My Company, Inc. to acquire the assets of the Company.

Terms and Estimated Purchase Price
$_____ to $_____ cash at closing. We would be willing to purchase

the Company without the purchase of the real estate and enter into a lease at current market rates and terms. In this case, our offer would range between $_____ and $_____.

Conditions of Transaction

1. We anticipate that an offer could be transacted, consummated, and closed within 90 days.

2. This proposal is subject to financing commitments that are satisfactory to us. We will be happy to provide you with references concerning our ability to finance the transaction.

3. Representations and warranties of seller with respect to accounts receivable, inventory, fixed assets, disclosure of liabilities, litigation, labor relations, corporate existence, etc., will be required.

4. We anticipate completing the due-diligence process within 30 to 45 days; and upon completion, we would want to move immediately to the execution of a Purchase and Sell Agreement.

5. If during the due-diligence process, we, at our sole discretion and judgment, wish to excuse ourselves from this transaction, we may do so without any liability, fee, penalty, or cost.

6. All fees and expenses of this transaction, including but not limited to legal, investment banking, accounting, broker, and due diligence, will be paid for by each of the respective parties.

Should you have any questions or concerns regarding this proposal, please feel free to contact me at _____.

Sincerely,

SELLING MEMORANDUM

Table of Contents

I. Conditions of Acceptance

This memorandum contains certain statements, estimates, and projections provided by Company B with respect to its anticipated future performance. Such statements, estimates, and projections reflect assumptions by Company B concerning anticipated results, which assumptions may or may not prove to be correct. No representations are made as to the accuracy of such statements, estimates, or projections.

Further, this section also uses strong language regarding the importance of keeping all confidential material confidential; and if there is a selling agent involved, that all communications relating to these materials should be directed to that agent. Management at Company B should not be contacted under any circumstances.

II. The Proposed Transaction

Recipients of this memorandum should determine their degree of interest in acquiring Company B. If, upon review of this information, it is decided that there is no further interest, it is requested that the memorandum be returned to _____. Such parties are reminded that they will continue to be bound by the Confidentiality Agreement.

Interested parties are asked to advise _____ of their interest, including a preliminary range of value and a suggested time frame for closing a transaction.

From those expressing interest, a small number will be invited to meet the management and tour the facility. Proposals will be invited from those making the tour, following which a buyer will be selected. Final negotiations will be concluded followed by a letter of intent, purchase and sell agreement, and a closing.

While price will be an important consideration, interested parties are advised that other conditions will also be important in selecting the successful bidder. Such conditions may include payment terms, timing, availability of necessary financing, etc.

III. Executive Summary/Company Profile

Company B

Any Street
Any Town, USA 11111

Ownership and Organization:
Business:
Financial Highlights:
Historical Performance and Projections:

IV. The Company

History:
Markets:
Products:
Competition:
Management:
Real Estate:

V. Financials

VI: Growth Strategies

Summary Investment Considerations:
Reason for Sell:

VII: Conclusion

PURCHASE AND SELL AGREEMENT

The purchase and sell agreement, also known as the P & S agreement or acquisition agreement, should contain the following characteristics:

1. It is a legally binding agreement.

2. The buyer will seek to protect himself or herself against such matters as pending litigation, environmental problems, and undisclosed liabilities.

3. The seller rarely sells for all cash; this leaves the buyer in a position to hold out on any future payments if the transaction is not what the seller represents it to be (also known as remedies).

4. The seller may opt for a lower price at closing for all cash than to risk post-closing adversity.

5. The representations and warranties area assures both parties of the legal and financial ability to consummate the transaction.

6. The covenants area of the agreement defines the obligations of the parties in respect to their conduct during the period between the signing and the closing

such as the seller's conducting the business in the ordinary course.

7. The indemnification section relates to discoveries after the closing.

8. The conditions area lists issues that must be satisfied before the parties become obligated to close the transaction.

APPENDIX G

REFERENCES

Russell, Robb. *Selling Your Business*, Streetwise Publication, Adams Media Corporation, 2002.

Russell, Robb. *Buying Your Own Business*, Adams Media Corporation, 1995.

Joseph, Richard A.; Anna M. Nekoranec; and Carl H. Stevens. *How to Buy a Business*, Dearborn Trade Publishing, 1993.

Albright, Mary; Carr, Clay. *101 Biggest Mistakes Managers Make, and How to Avoid Them*, Prentice Hall Publishing, 1997.

Fulton, Roger. *Common Sense Supervision*, Ten Speed Press, 1988.

Drucker, Peter F. *Management Challenges for the 21st Century*, Harper Collins Publishers, 1999.

INDEX

I

R ene' Richards is a published author and writer
of business and finance articles for readers across
educational and entrepreneurial boundaries. She
and her family live in rural Alabama where she is a practicing
accountant and financial services advisor. This book, "*How
to Buy and/or Sell a Small Business for Maximum Profit,*" is a
walk-through of the process most often encountered by small
businesses in the transfer from one great dreamer to another!

MORE GREAT TITLES FROM ATLANTIC PUBLISHING

ONLINE MARKETING SUCCESS STORIES: INSIDER SECRETS FROM THE EXPERTS WHO ARE MAKING MILLIONS ON THE INTERNET TODAY

Standing out in the turmoil of today's Internet marketplace is a major challenge. There are many books and courses on Internet marketing; this is the only book that will provide you with insider secrets. We asked the marketing experts who make their living on the Internet every day—and they talked. *Online Marketing Success Stories* will give you real-life examples of how successful businesses market their products online. The information is so useful that you can read a page and put the idea into action—today!

With e-commerce expected to reach $40 billion and online businesses anticipated to increase by 500 percent through 2010, your business needs guidance from today's successful Internet marketing veterans. Learn the most efficient ways to bring consumers to your site, get visitors to purchase, how to up-sell, oversights to avoid, and how to steer clear of years of disappointment.

We spent thousands of hours interviewing, e-mailing, and communicating with hundreds of today's most successful
e-commerce marketers. This book not only chronicles their achievements, but is a compilation of their secrets and proven successful ideas. If you are interested in learning hundreds of hints, tricks, and secrets on how to make money (or more money) with your Web site, then this book is for you.

Instruction is great, but advice from experts is even better, and the experts chronicled in this book are earning millions. This new exhaustively researched book will provide you with a jam-packed assortment of innovative ideas that you can put to use today. This book gives you the proven strategies, innovative ideas, and actual case studies to help you sell more with less time and effort.

288 Pages • Item # OMS-02 • $21.95

To order call 1-800-814-1132 or visit www.atlantic-pub.com

2,001 Innovative Ways to Save Your Company Thousands by Reducing Costs: A Complete Guide to Creative Cost Cutting and Boosting Profits

For the small business owner, every dollar you can save by reducing costs goes directly to the bottom line in increased profits. This new book details over 2,000 specific ways that your company can reduce costs today. This is not a "theory" book; there is practical advice on thousands of innovative ways to cut costs in every area of your business. Not only is the idea presented, but the pertinent information is provided such as contact information and Web sites for companies, products, or services recommended.

You will discover over 2,000 practical insider techniques and tips that have been gleaned from successful business operators from around the world and tested in real-life business applications. You can put this information in place today to reduce expenses and expand profits. Easy to read and understand, this step-by-step guide will take the mystery out of how to reduce costs in several critical areas: office, operations, labor, cost of goods sold, advertising, marketing, human resources, insurance, employee benefits, compensation, pension plans, training, accounting, software, Web site, mailing, shipping and receiving, rent, interest and debt, utilities, and hundreds more.   **288 Pages • Item # IWS-02 • $21.95**

365 Foolish Mistakes Smart Managers Make Every Day: How and Why to Avoid Them

Here's a very surprising statistic: Within the first 18 months on the job, 40 percent of all management newcomers fail by either getting fired, quitting, or receiving a bad review, according to Manchester Inc., a business consulting group. Some first-timers are overwhelmed by their newfound power while some are weighed down by the responsibility. But for most, the overriding concern is to avoid personal failure.

This new groundbreaking book will guide the new manager to success and avoid the many common mistakes and pitfalls along the way. You will learn how to face the unique challenges every day in your job and offer detailed and innovative solutions to help you achieve your potential. Learn how to become a true leader who commands respect, commitment, and credibility.

288 Pages • Item # FMS-02 • $21.95

To order call 1-800-814-1132 or visit www.atlantic-pub.com

365 Answers About Human Resources for the Small Business Owner: What Every Manager Needs to Know About Workplace Law

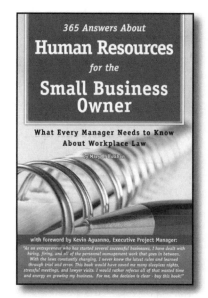

Finally there is a complete and up-to-date resource for the small business owner. Tired of high legal and consulting fees? This new book is your answer! Detailed are over 300 common questions employers have about employees and the law; it's like having an employment attorney on your staff.

Topics include: equal employment opportunity, age discrimination, Americans with Disabilities Act (ADA), workers or applicants with AIDS, unacceptable job performance, termination, substance abuse, drug and alcohol testing, safety, harassment, compensation policies, job classifications, recordkeeping, overtime, employee performance evaluations, wage and salary reviews, payroll deductions, reduction in wages, pay periods, payroll advances, wage garnishment, severance pay, unemployment compensation, operating policies, ethical standards, open-door policy, suggestions and customer feedback, smoke-free workplace, dress code, work schedule, flexible scheduling, telecommuting, absenteeism, tardiness, confidentiality, employee privacy, electronic communication, responsible use of equipment, e-mail and Internet, prohibited content, copyrighted materials, responsible use of cell phones, security procedures, telephone usage, use of company vehicles, solicitation for outside causes, outside employment, personnel files, release of information, access to files, possession of weapons, improper personal conduct, company benefits, time off, holidays, vacations, sick leave policies, bereavement, jury duty, education and training, leaves of absence, Family and Medical Leave Act, personal or medical leaves not required by law, military leave, insurance, on-the-job accidents or injuries, medical/life insurance, flexible benefit plans, pension, and profit sharing.

288 Pages • Item # HRM-02 • $21.95

To order call 1-800-814-1132 or visit www.atlantic-pub.com

365 Ways to Motivate and Reward Your Employees Every Day—With Little or No Money

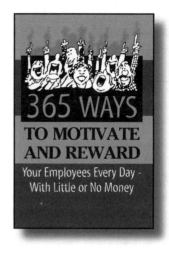

"I LOVE my job!" Is that what your employees are saying? Sadly, according to the U.S. Department of Labor Statistics, American businesses lost an average of 25 days of work in 2001 due to employee anxiety and stress. Don't let your business become part of this dismal statistic. You can improve employee morale and create a harmonious workplace, which will increase profits and productivity.

This new book is packed with hundreds of simple and inexpensive ways to motivate, challenge, and reward your employees. Employees today need constant re-enforcement and recognition—and here's how to do it. This is not a "theory" book. You will find real-life, proven examples and case studies from actual companies that you can put to use immediately. You can use this book daily to boost morale, productivity, and profits. This is your opportunity to build an organization that people love to work at with these quick, effective, humorous, innovative, and simply fun solutions to employee work challenges. Make your business a happy place to work, and reap the benefits.   **288 Pages • Item # 365-01 • $24.95**

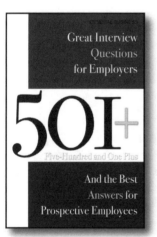

501+ Great Interview Questions for Employers and the Best Answers for Prospective Employees

For anyone who hires employees, this is a must-have book. It is also essential for anyone searching for a new job or going on a job interview.

Hiring new employees to fill a job vacancy is one of any manager's most important responsibilities. This new book contains a wide variety of carefully worded questions that will help make the employee search easier. These questions can help you determine a candidate's personality type, the type of work he or she is best suited for, and if the person will mesh with your existing employees and workplace. Once you learn the right questions to ask, you'll get the best employees.

As you know, it is not always the best candidate that gets the job—but often the person who interviews the best. For the prospective employee, learn how to sell yourself and get the job you want! From this new book you will learn how to answer the toughest interview questions by being fully prepared and understand what employers are looking for.

288 Pages • Item # 501-02 • $24.95

To order call 1-800-814-1132 or visit www.atlantic-pub.com

DESIGN YOUR OWN EFFECTIVE EMPLOYEE HANDBOOK: HOW TO MAKE THE MOST OF YOUR STAFF—WITH COMPANION CD-ROM

If you have employees, you need employment policies in writing distributed to every employee. The U.S. Supreme Court has ruled that businesses can protect themselves against damages and liability against employee lawsuits by providing clear, written policies covering the rights and responsibilities of their employees.

Our Employee Handbook Template is the ideal solution to produce your own handbook in less than an hour. The companion CD-ROM in MS Word contains the template, which you can easily edit for our own purposes; just fill in the blank. The book discusses various options you may have in developing the policies. Our employee handbook has been edited and approved by lawyers specializing in employment law. Developing your own handbook now couldn't be easier or less expensive!

Topics include: equal employment opportunity, age discrimination, Americans with Disabilities Act (ADA), workers or applicants with AIDS, unacceptable job performance, termination, substance abuse, drug and alcohol testing, safety, harassment, compensation policies, job classifications, recordkeeping, overtime, employee performance evaluations, wage and salary reviews, payroll deductions, reduction in wages, pay periods, payroll advances, wage garnishment, severance pay, unemployment compensation, operating policies, ethical standards, open-door policy, smoke-free workplace, dress code, flexible scheduling, telecommuting, absenteeism, tardiness, confidentiality, employee privacy, electronic communication, responsible use of equipment, e-mail and Internet, prohibited content, copyrighted materials, responsible use of cell phones, security procedures, telephone usage, use of company vehicles, solicitation for outside causes, outside employment, personnel files, release of information, access to files, possession of weapons, improper personal conduct, company benefits, time off, holidays, vacations, sick leave policies, bereavement, jury duty, education and training, leaves of absence, Family and Medical Leave Act, personal or medical leaves not required by law, military leave, insurance, on-the-job accidents or injuries, medical/life insurance, flexible benefit plans, pension, and profit sharing.

288 Pages • Item # GEH-02 • $39.95 with Companion CD-ROM

To order call 1-800-814-1132 or visit www.atlantic-pub.com

How to Hire, Train & Keep the Best Employees for Your Small Business: With Companion CD-ROM

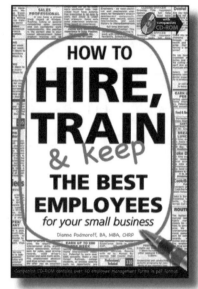

Getting the right people in the right job and then getting them to stay are the key elements in effective business organizations. It sounds straightforward, and many business-people simply put an ad in the paper, wait for the applications to arrive, do some interviewing, and then hire the people they liked the best. Boom, done! Then all hell starts breaking loose: there are attendance problems, attitude problems, and personality conflicts; the business is suffering; the employees are suffering; and management is barely able to keep the ship afloat. What went wrong?

The short answer is they hired the wrong people; they failed to make human resource management a priority. The good news is that careful planning and strategic management of the recruitment, hiring and retention processes will greatly improve success; the bad news is that HR management is not an exact science because people are unpredictable. Fortunately, there are many strategies, techniques and practices proven to improve all aspects of people management.

These are the skills you'll learn in How to Hire, Train & Keep the Best Employees for Your Small Business. This book covers all the essential elements of employee management in an easy-to-understand and practical manner. Topics include:

- Successful Recruitment Strategies—how to find good, potential employees.
- Hiring and Interviewing—asking the right questions, the right way.
- Effective Communication—giving and receiving information effectively.
- Training—improving employee performance.
- Motivation—creating job satisfaction.
- Leadership and Team-Building—influencing employees to work effectively.

The companion CD-ROM contains dozens of employee training and human resource forms including: unique employment applications, interview questions and analysis, reference checks, work schedules, rules to live by, reporting forms, confidentially agreement, and an extensive human resource audit form. Simply print out any form you need, when you need it.

288 Pages • Item # HTK-02 • $29.95

To order call 1-800-814-1132 or visit www.atlantic-pub.com